SHARMAN ON BASKETBALL SHOOTING

SHARMAN

by Bill

PRENTICE-HALL INC ENGLEWOOD CLIFFS N J

ON BASKETBALL

SHOOTING

Sharman

Library of Congress Catalog Card No.: 65-15561

80776—B C

To my head coach, Ileana, and our four assistants, Jerry, Nancy, Janice, and Tommy; also to my most loyal fans, Mom and Dad.

Rebounding, passing and defense may be important aspects of basketball. But the entire game still revolves around putting the ball through the hole. If he can't impress the coach with his shooting, the average player never gets a chance to display his other talents.

In my opinion, there is no one in the game better qualified than Bill Sharman to advise the reader wanting to improve his shooting technique. Sharman is the most accurate shooter I have ever seen and he approaches shooting as a student and a perfectionist. Not every reader will have Sharman's native ability, but the important thing is that he use every bit of his own potential. This book will help the reader do this.

Bill Sharman *personifies* winning basketball, and I'm sure that his advice in this book will pave the way to better shooting and better basketball.

ACKNOWLEDGMENTS

I would like to express sincere gratitude to the many people who have made this book possible. A special thanks is extended to Diann Laing for the art work, to Frank Starnes for his help, friendship, and technical assistance, and to Glenn Wilkes for his aid in the final preparation of the manuscript.

The book received a tremendous contribution from the "super stars" who allowed me to interview them and print some of the secrets that have made them All-Time Greats of the game.

Others who have offered valuable help in the preparation are Jack Barry of the Boston *Globe*, who provided pictures from his files; Carolyn Winston, secretarial assistance; Rosemary Ruzicka and Glayde DeKay, extra correspondence; Mrs. Jerry Walker, typing; and Dennis McCarbrey, photography.

Most of the players' pictures were furnished by the teams in the N.B.A. I want to thank the following publicity people: Howie McHugh of the Boston

Celtics, Gil Smith of the Los Angeles *Lakers*, Steve Hoffman of the Cincinnati *Royals*, Lester Scott of the New York *Knickerbockers*, Dan McGuire of the San Francisco *Warriors*, George Maskin of the Detroit *Pistons*, Harvey Pollack of the Philadelphia *76ers*, Marty Blake of the St. Louis *Hawks*, and Jerry Krause of the Baltimore *Bullets*.

CONTENTS

SHARMAN ON BASKETBALL SHOOTING

I

DEVELOPING CORRECT SHOOTING

HABITS

He wins who scores more points than his opponent in basketball, and shooting is the backbone of the game. Regardless of what else takes place on the court, accurate shooting is a must if a team is to become and remain a strong contender. Outstanding ball handling and dribbling, colorful patterns, rebounding—all are wasted if a team cannot consistently rip the net.

A coach should establish a definite *philosophy* of shooting early in his coaching career, a philosophy that will serve to guide the teaching of shooting skills, the planning and conduct of practice sessions, and game strategy. In the following paragraphs is presented my own basic shooting philosophy, developed from my many years as a player and coach in college and professional basketball.

First Shots Are Critical

It is tremendously important that players establish correct shooting habits at the start, for whatever a player practices becomes habitual to him. It takes five times more work to break a bad habit than it does to develop a good one.

A coach must make certain that he teaches his players good shooting technique, and he must require that it be practiced correctly at all times. Practice of "fancy" or "trick" shots is out. Whenever possible, shooting drills should approximate game conditions. In a regular game, the shooter will have his opponent's hand in his face 95 per cent of the time, so in practice, I put a man with his hands up in front of the shooter.

Stars Are Made—Not Born

Good shooters are developed, not born. I doubt that there has ever been a great shooter who did not require countless hours of practice to develop his proficiency. True, great hitters in baseball, great passers in football, and great shooters in basketball have to be blessed with muscular coordination before their full potential can be developed. Naturally, there is a limit to the proficiency any man can develop, but assuming a boy has good coordination, a genuine interest in basketball, and a sincere desire to improve, he can be helped a great deal. Give him understanding of sound techniques, and improvement will come with proper practice.

Know the Target Area

The shooter must concentrate on his target area— the point on the rim or backboard at which he is sighting—even after the ball is released. Failure to concentrate on the target area is a common shooting fault, particularly among young players. Be on the alert to correct it. I require that each player know, for every shot he misses, just where the ball hit the rim. Knowing where the ball hit, he can quickly see where his target area should have been. A boy hits the front rim, sees that he is short, realizes he must move his target back; if his shot is to the side, he sees he must move his target area toward the opposite side; and so on.

The Percentage Shot

Among the fundamental shooting skills is knowing *when to shoot*. All players love to shoot and, to *their* minds, seldom take a bad shot. It is the coach's difficult task to make certain that each player comes to know the floor areas from which he can shoot with a winning percentage of hits and the phases of the team offense from which those shots will be obtained. Players must learn the difference between the good shot and the bad, and the importance of taking the good shot. A boy works free and shoots five feet from the basket, but he is off balance—he rushes the shot and is jerky. Whether or not he hits, that boy has taken a bad shot. In contrast, a boy shooting 20 feet from the basket, who is on balance and in control of his body, releases a smooth, rhythmic shot that will produce a high percentage of hits.

I have come to the conclusion that every bad shot taken actually costs a team about half a point. Clearly, the coach must stress over and over again the importance of knowing when to shoot and whether or not a shot will be good or bad. So many games are decided by one or two points that just a couple of bad shots per game can make a difference of three or four victories a season.

It is important that players be aware of the significance of percentage shooting. The idea is not to cause players worry over a low percentage—rather, each player should come to know what his percentage potentials are from various areas on the floor. The coach should point out to the boy who can shoot 40 per cent from 20 feet but only 20 per cent from 25 feet that he should refrain from taking 25-foot shots. But it is up to the coach to use that boy within the patterns in such a way as to take full advantage of his 40 per cent potential.

It is proved over and over again that teams with high shooting percentages are strong contenders and consistent winners. Percentage shooting can be taught, and it goes hand in hand with teaching the good shot. The team that shoots percentage is taking the good shot.

Practice Areas

From what areas on the floor should players practice their shots? It is my belief that college and professional players should specialize in shooting areas. For high school and junior high players, shots from several areas should be stressed according to the preference of the coach. The young novice is not ready to specialize—he should shoot from the guard, forward, and center positions.

In many instances, the team offense will dictate those floor areas from which players should practice their shots. One offense may not let a forward shot from the guard position, but another offense will—the shuffle offense, for example, swings the post man out to the top of the circle for the shot. The coach should analyze his offense and guide his players to practice in those areas they will shoot from in actual play.

Planning Practice Sessions

Practice sessions afford the best opportunity for both individual and team improvements; they should, therefore, be planned in detail to assure maximum results. Planning should be done with the aid of some kind of master guide. Drill should be varied and progressive—it is most important that drill does not become boring to the players.

A *minimum* of 30 minutes, preferably during the first part of each practice session, should be devoted to shooting. Shooting practice should not be haphazard; it should be as well planned as the other phases of practice. No drill should require players to shoot from positions they would not shoot from in actual games, and shooting drills should be determined by the type of offense the team uses.

Basketball practice should capture the flavor of game conditions as closely as possible—and that means competitive drills. The element of competition affords game-condition practice and it makes practice interesting to the players—the more so if winners are rewarded.

Developing Complete Players

Shooting, in my opinion, is the most important skill in the game, but I emphasize the importance of developing *complete* basketball players. Too often I have seen a good shooter fail to make the team because he couldn't perform other important skills satisfactorily. The complete player knows not only how and when to shoot, but also how to dribble, pass, play defense—in short, how to perform all the skills required for a championship team. The complete player is not developed in a few weeks. Hours and hours of dedicated practice are the price of every skill. To make himself a complete player, a boy must be willing to work and work hard to overcome his weakness as well as to perfect his strengths. He must be willing to dedicate himself to the game; he must *want* to excel.

A coach, therefore, should clearly establish—and set his teaching procedures by—a sound, basic shooting philosophy. He must examine it from time to time and be ready to alter it as new developments come along. And he should share this philosophy with his players!

2

ANATOMY OF A SHOT

The proper shooting technique for any type of shot requires the coordination of certain interrelated fundamentals. Each fundamental is so dependent on a number of others that it is difficult to say which is more important. A shooter may exhibit correct stance, grip, sighting, and so on, but his shot will often go astray if his elbow is out of position. The same would be true if the elbow were in position but the shooter was guilty of, say, improper grip or poor sighting of the target area.

What Makes a Shot Hit

The following ingredients are absolutely essential to make a goal, regardless of the type of shot. They are discussed thoroughly in the rest of the chapter:

1. Body balance and control
2. Stance

3. Grip
4. Position of elbow
5. Position of the ball before release
6. Sighting the basket and target areas
7. Release of the ball
8. Force behind the shot
9. Follow-through
10. Flight arc of ball
11. Concentration

Body balance and control

Body balance is critical in all phases of basketball; it is especially so in shooting. An off-balance shot generally is a bad shot, and bad shots lose ball games. Body control is achieved by shifting one's center of gravity to maintain balance at all times. The player who maintains his center of gravity too high is top-heavy and cannot control his body movements. A center of gravity maintained too low causes a shooter to become cramped or tied up, unable to move freely. Body balance is vital to the smooth, rhythmic, flowing motion so necessary to consistently good shooting. Little effort is needed to shoot from a proper base.

Bob Cousy, for instance, seemed to have extraperceptive body control. Dribbling, fast-breaking, changing direction, changing pace, passing behind his back, doing some extraordinary thing only he could do— no matter what the maneuver, Cousy always wound up on balance. Body control *depends* on body balance.

Big men should work to quicken their responses and movements, for they are often the most indifferent to body balance and control. Big centers particularly incline to be rigid and awkward; their biggest problem seems to be learning to keep the knees flexed. It is especially important for big men in bas-

BODY BALANCE AND CONTROL

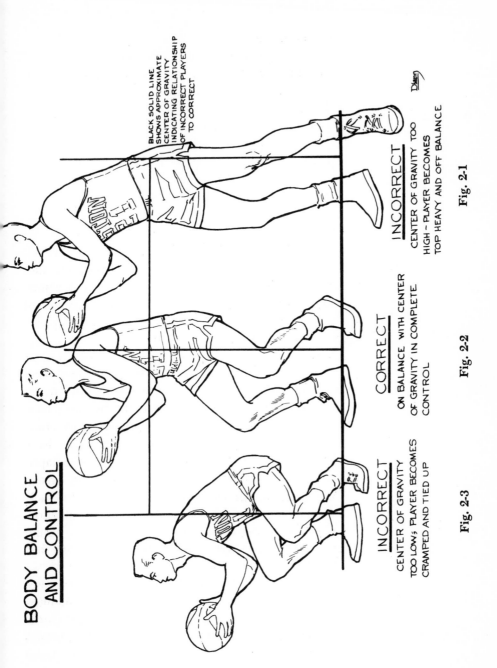

BLACK SOLID LINE SHOWS APPROXIMATE CENTER OF GRAVITY INDICATING RELATIONSHIP OF INCORRECT PLAYERS TO CORRECT

INCORRECT
CENTER OF GRAVITY TOO LOW; PLAYER BECOMES CRAMPED AND TIED UP

Fig. 2-3

CORRECT
ON BALANCE WITH CENTER OF GRAVITY IN COMPLETE CONTROL

Fig. 2-2

INCORRECT
CENTER OF GRAVITY TOO HIGH – PLAYER BECOMES TOP HEAVY AND OFF BALANCE

Fig. 2-1

29

ketball to learn how to maintain the center of gravity at the proper position for best balance and maximum responsiveness, especially for shooting. Any player— big or not—who doesn't have proper body balance and perfect body control will cost his team many points during his career.

A series of line drawings has been included depicting proper and improper body balance when shooting. Figure 2-1 shows that the shooter's center of gravity is too high, leaving him top-heavy and certainly not balanced or in control of his body. Figure 2-2 shows the shooter in perfect balance, in excellent posture to move quickly and shoot accurately. In Figure 2-3, the shooter's center of gravity is too low—he is too cramped to move quickly or to shoot with accuracy.

Stance

The feet play a very important role in shooting—a shot properly executed really comes as much off the tips of the toes as off the tips of the fingers. In the one-hand set shot, a right-handed shooter's right foot is his front (forward) foot; the left-handed shooter's left foot is his front foot (see Figure 2-4). As shown in the drawing, the front foot points toward the basket, and the back foot is placed at a 30- to 45-degree angle. The feet are approximately shoulders' width apart. Knees are flexed—the greater the shooter's distance from the basket, the more the knees are flexed and the body crouched, to get maximum force and power from the legs. A shooter closer to the basket needs less power, thus he need not flex his knees as much. I would encourage players to experiment with the shooting distance-stance relationship to find out what is best for them individually.

STANCE

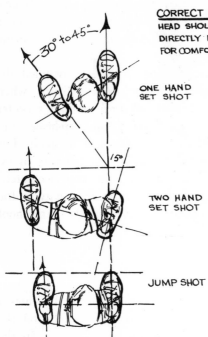

CORRECT HEAD AND FEET POSITION — THE HEAD SHOULD BE IN THE MIDDLE AND DIRECTLY BETWEEN THE FEET ON ALL SHOTS FOR COMFORT AND BALANCE

30° to 45°

ONE HAND SET SHOT

IF RIGHT HANDED THE RIGHT FOOT SHOULD BE FORWARD AND POINTING TOWARD BASKET, THE LEFT FOOT IS BACK AND POINTING OUT AT APPROXIMATELY 30° TO 45° ANGLE

15°

TWO HAND SET SHOT

USUALLY THE LEFT FOOT IS SLIGHTLY FORWARD OF THE RIGHT FOOT. FEET SHOULD BE SPREAD ENOUGH TO BE COMFORTABLE AND ON BALANCE

JUMP SHOT

FEET SHOULD BE LINED UP ALMOST PERPENDICULAR, APPROXIMATELY THE SAME WIDTH AS THE SHOULDERS THE DESIRED STANCE IS FORMED BY THE STRONGEST JUMPING POSITION

INCORRECT HEAD POSITION

WHEN HEAD POSITION IS TOO FAR FORWARD OR BACKWARD BETWEEN THE FEET, IT WILL PLACE THE PLAYER IN AN AWKWARD AND OFF-BALANCE POSITION

Diann

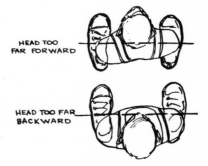

HEAD TOO FAR FORWARD

HEAD TOO FAR BACKWARD

Fig. 2-4

PROPER GRIP

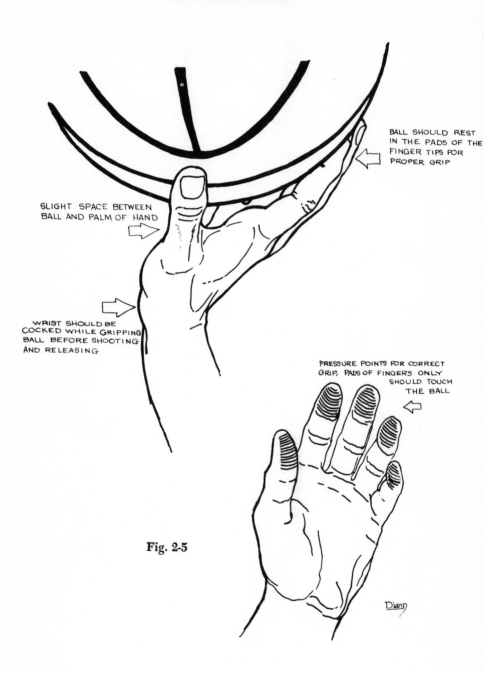

BALL SHOULD REST IN THE PADS OF THE FINGER TIPS FOR PROPER GRIP

SLIGHT SPACE BETWEEN BALL AND PALM OF HAND

WRIST SHOULD BE COCKED WHILE GRIPPING BALL BEFORE SHOOTING AND RELEASING

PRESSURE POINTS FOR CORRECT GRIP, PADS OF FINGERS ONLY SHOULD TOUCH THE BALL

Fig. 2-5

Dian

The grip

The ball should be touched only by the fingertips
—never by the palm of the hand. The fingers should
be spread in a natural, relaxed position—I stress the
importance of comfortable finger contact with the
ball. Stand behind the shooter to check his hand-
elbow-arm alignment (see Figure 2-5). The fingers of
the left hand touch the underside of the ball merely
to ease the burden on the right hand (Figure 2-6).
The left hand functions somewhat as a tee holds a
golf ball. The two hands work together to start the
ball in a lifting motion. It is important not to allow
the elbows to get in too close to the sides of the body
or the left hand to get down too far on the ball; such
a position will tighten the shoulders and accuracy will
be lost. The fingertips, the Vee, the wrist cock, the
elbow position, the left hand, and the fingerspread—
all are shown in Figure 2-6 (see next page).

Position of elbow

The position of the elbow of the shooting arm is
very important: it should be natural, it should be
comfortable, and it should be almost directly *under*
the ball. For some reason when beginners start shooting they often get the elbow to point out sideways
from the body instead of toward the basket. This is
an unnatural position. There is a simple way to illustrate this. Extend the shooting arm upward toward
the basket: the elbow naturally points directly at it!
(See Figure 2-7, page 35.)

A controlled elbow helps produce a steady, accurate
shot. If the elbow is held too close to the body or
pointed inward, it will create a cramped shoulder position and accuracy will be lost. To get correct position,

GRIP

INCORRECT

CORRECT

BALL SHOULD BE HELD
IN FINGER TIPS, WELL
BALANCED BETWEEN
THUMB AND FINGERS
IN V POSITION.
FINGERS SHOULD BE
SPREAD IN COMFORTABLE
POSITION FOR MAXIMUM
SHOOTING ACCURACY

INCORRECT

Diann

Fig. 2-6

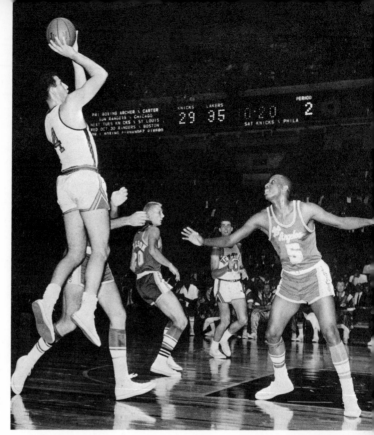

Fig. 2-7: A good example of pointing the elbow at the target. The shooter is Art Heyman of the *Knickerbockers*, guarded by the *Lakers'* Dick Barnett.

the elbow should be fairly close to the body and in line with the basket.

A personal technique I have concentrated on many times involves having the elbow come up first as the shot is started and point it right at the basket. As the shot is started, the ball is moved upward and back toward the shoulder. The elbow moves forward toward the basket, ahead of the ball and under it. The arm folds like a hinge, giving good leverage. When the arm is extended in the execution of the shot, the "hinge" unfolds effortlessly but with control and rhythm, snapped forward and downward, giving the ball a good backspin.

If the elbow were kept behind the ball throughout the shot, the wrist could not be cocked back far enough, and the ball would be *pushed*—somewhat as a knuckleball is in baseball—not properly *shot*.

POSITION OF BALL AND ELBOW

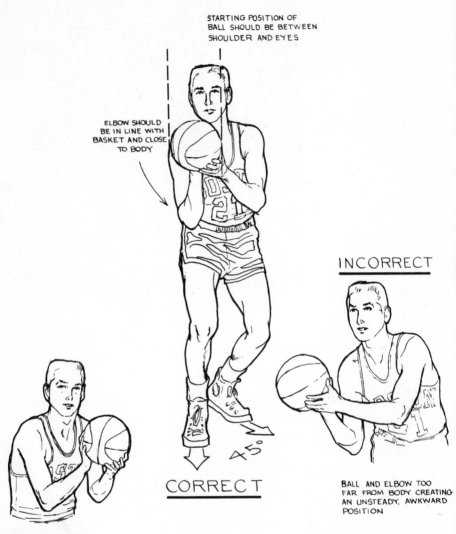

STARTING POSITION OF
BALL SHOULD BE BETWEEN
SHOULDER AND EYES

ELBOW SHOULD
BE IN LINE WITH
BASKET AND CLOSE
TO BODY

45°

CORRECT

INCORRECT

BALL AND ELBOW TOO
FAR FROM BODY CREATING
AN UNSTEADY, AWKWARD
POSITION

ELBOW AND BALL TOO
FAR IN FRONT OF BODY
WHICH HINDERS FREE
AND RELAXED ACTION

INCORRECT

Fig. 2-8

Diann

Position of ball

The ball should be held close to the body prior to the shot. Holding the ball too far away creates a feeling of unsteadiness, and the shooter seems to have less control over the ball. So the ball can be sighted before it is released, I recommend that it be held somewhere between the shoulders and the eyes. The point to remember is that any position used should be *comfortable*, regardless of the style used by the shooter.

Actually, the ball can be held properly anywhere from the hips to a position above the head. To illustrate two extremes of shooting, let's look at Bob Cousy and former N.B.A. star Mel Hutchins. Cousy holds the ball in the vicinity of the hips because he feels this gives him greater extension of the arm, and he can shoot more accurately from farther out. Hutchins held the ball over his head to start the shot. Both of these outstanding ball players observed the fundamentals, and both styles were effective. I personally prefer to hold the ball up around the shoulders (see Fig. 2-8) because it gives me more control over the ball and allows me to keep the ball closer to my eyes so that I can sight it somewhat as a rifleman does.

Sighting the basket and target area

This phase of shooting is too often overlooked. A shooter usually looks at the basket prior to making his shot. But that does not mean he sees a target area. It is possible to look at an object without really seeing it in depth.

To see a target area in depth it is necessary to know exactly where in the basket area the target should be, to stare at it, and to memorize the image. I recom-

TARGET AREA

ALWAYS AIM FOR CENTER OF RIM

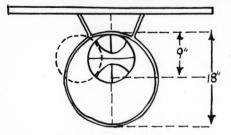

BALL APPROXIMATELY 9" INCHES
IN DIAMETER, RIM 18" INCHES
IN DIAMETER, THIS LEAVES
9" INCHES MARGIN OF ERROR

IF BALL IS AIMED STRAIGHT IN THE MIDDLE OF THE
RIM, IT THEN HAS 9" INCHES MARGIN OF ERROR.
IF BALL IS SLIGHTLY OFF CENTER THEN MARGIN
OF ERROR IS LOST OR GREATLY REDUCED

3 REASONS TO AIM FOR BACK OF RIM

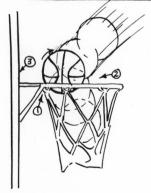

① - IF BALL HITS BACK EDGE OF RIM THE
PROPER BACK SPIN WILL HELP FORCE
BALL DOWNWARD INTO BASKET

② - IF BALL IS SHORT OF TARGET, IT STILL
HAS APPROXIMATELY 9" INCHES MARGIN
OF ERROR IF KEPT IN CENTER OF RIM

③ - IF BALL IS LONG OF TARGET, IT STILL
HAS A CHANCE OF BANKING OFF THE
BACKBOARD

Diann

Fig. 2-9

mend that a player get out on the court and, from
different areas on the floor, just concentrate on the
basket and pick out the target areas that should be
aimed at. He should try to carry these mental images
over into the ball game.

A target area is comparable to a small bull's-eye in a rifle target. I personally feel it should be somewhere on the back part of the rim, and especially in the middle. There are several reasons for this. First, if there is proper backspin on the ball, and the ball should hit a back portion of the rim, the ball will be forced into the basket. Second, the ball is approximately nine inches in diameter; the rim is 18 inches in diameter. Theoretically, if the ball is aimed at the middle of the back part of the rim, there is approximately a nine-inch margin for error. Third, a long, straight shot hitting the back part of the rim on top will bounce up, hit the backboard and—with a bit of luck—fall through the hoop. In golf, the ball has no chance to drop into the cup if it is short. The same principle applies in basketball, so keep the ball to the deep part of the basket (see Figure 2-9).

The only time I advocate using the backboard for a target is for close-in shots. If the backboard were used as the target, the actual target area would be different for every position on the floor from which a shot might be taken. But in close to the basket the backboard should be used on hook shots, full-speed lay-ups, and short jumpers from the side. If there is a magic circle inside of which the backboard is best used, it is perhaps for any shot made within 10 feet of the basket. Sam Jones of the Boston *Celtics*, however, is an exceptionally good shooter, and quite often uses the backboard from 15 to 20 feet out.

Release of ball

If the ball is to be released properly, the shot must be started properly. The effort for any shot starts in the feet and works up through the wrist, and finally through the fingertips. Shooters should try to avoid jerky, hurried shooting motions because timing, accuracy, and control will be thrown off.

At the start of the shot the shooter should dip the ball slightly. Then, as the ball is started upward, the elbow moves under the ball so that the ball is coming upward and backward rather than toward the basket. As the ball moves backward and the wrist cocks, the elbow should be completely under the ball and in front of it. This will allow the elbow to act as a hinge. The leverage in the elbow and in the wrist will permit a smooth, soft release because so little effort is needed.

As the ball is started forward toward the basket, the elbow unlocks, then the wrist is uncocked. The ball should roll off the fingertips with a lot of backspin—backspin is the product of proper wrist action. It is very important that the ball not be pushed toward the basket with a stiff wrist action. The hand and fingers then move under the ball and downward in proper follow-through.

Jerry West and Oscar Robertson keep their elbows way under the ball, hold the ball high, and get maximum wrist snap into their shots. These two stars exemplify very well the correct wrist and elbow position before the ball is released.

I emphasize a very strong wrist snap, including a complete follow-through in which the wrist and fingers are extended in a downward and outward movement. The outward movement of the wrist and fingers is important to counteract the natural inward movement of the wrist when it is flexed forward. Any inward movement of the wrist and fingers will impart sidespin instead of backspin to the ball (see Figure 2-10).

It is very important to use the legs and body so that the arm and wrist do not have to furnish all the muscle needed to get the shot to the basket. When the force behind the shot is generated from the legs and body,

RELEASE OF BALL

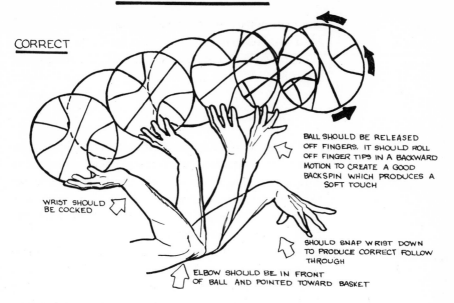

CORRECT

BALL SHOULD BE RELEASED
OFF FINGERS, IT SHOULD ROLL
OFF FINGER TIPS IN A BACKWARD
MOTION TO CREATE A GOOD
BACKSPIN WHICH PRODUCES A
SOFT TOUCH

WRIST SHOULD
BE COCKED

SHOULD SNAP WRIST DOWN
TO PRODUCE CORRECT FOLLOW
THROUGH

ELBOW SHOULD BE IN FRONT
OF BALL AND POINTED TOWARD BASKET

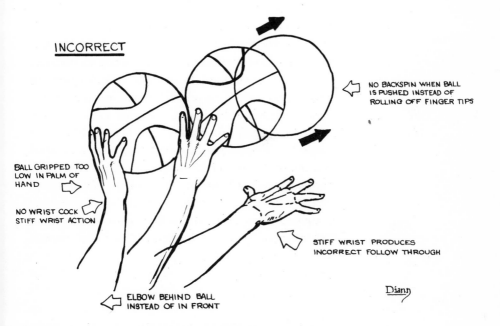

INCORRECT

NO BACKSPIN WHEN BALL
IS PUSHED INSTEAD OF
ROLLING OFF FINGER TIPS

BALL GRIPPED TOO
LOW IN PALM OF
HAND

NO WRIST COCK
STIFF WRIST ACTION

STIFF WRIST PRODUCES
INCORRECT FOLLOW THROUGH

Diann

ELBOW BEHIND BALL
INSTEAD OF IN FRONT

Fig. 2-10

41

the total power and momentum enables the arm to extend in a relaxed manner. The elbow and wrist snap should merely accentuate the momentum started in the legs.

Force behind the shot

The power of interaction, or momentum behind the shot, is a summation of forces, a chain of events in which forces build up in such a way that when one force reaches its peak another force takes over. The initial force is generated by the push-off from the feet—the summation builds up through the interactions of the body until it is released as an explosion of forces at the end of the extended arm. The key force behind the shot is the crouched position, the bending of the knees. Probably the most common fault of basketball players is that they try to push the ball. They try to generate power behind the shot with their arms rather than with their legs and bodies. If the legs and body are not used correctly or adequately in the shot, the arm will be strained. When the ball is released, the arms will not be able to follow through in a natural and relaxed manner. The longer the shot a player must shoot, the more he should bend his knees. From a low crouch the shooter will be able to generate great force with relatively little effort, imposing little strain on his shooting arm. For long shots—anything 18 feet or more from the basket—he should spring up so vigorously as to leave the floor. Naturally, if he is in closer he doesn't need as much power or force, so he will not have to bend or crouch as low.

Follow-through

I feel that correct follow-through is absolutely essential to accuracy and control in shooting. Unfortunately, one of the most common faults of less experienced players is failure to use a complete follow-through.

I strongly advocate an exaggerated, relaxed follow-through at all times. As the ball is released, the wrist should snap down and slightly outward. The arm should be fully extended also. A good instance of an exaggerated follow-through and its importance to the outcome of a shot is exemplified in golf. Golfers claim that after the ball is hit the follow-through should continue for at least a couple of feet in the ball's line of flight. The same principle applies in basketball, although the extension is not carried as far as it is in golf.

Flight arc of the ball

One of the most controversial aspects of basketball shooting has centered around the flight arc of the ball: should the ball be given a high or a low arc? One advantage of a high arc is that the ball, being high in the air, descends at a steep angle toward the basket. The steeper the angle, the wider the margin for error and the greater the possibility of making the basket. A low arc lets the shooter move the ball straighter toward the target.

I strongly advocate that most beginners use a medium arc of, say, 35–45 degrees. Once a player has gained some experience and confidence, he can experiment to see just what arc he feels most comfortable with.

The medium arc seems to allow a shooter better control. I believe it is possible to consistently place the ball in the middle of the basket with a medium arc, and this is definitely an advantage for a high shooting percentage. Every player should learn how to control the arc in relation to his intended target. When shots are short of the target, a *lower* arc will usually help get the ball back deeper in or on the rim. If a shooter is consistently hitting long, a *higher* arc will help reduce his distance to the target he is normally aiming at.

Concentration

The ability to concentrate during the fast pace of a ball game is quite important. A good basketball player should always have the entire picture of the ball and its surroundings. It is extremely important to know where one's teammates are before taking a shot. It is even more important to know where the defensive man is before deciding whether to shoot, pass, or dribble. A defensive man may move in on a player as he is dribbling, or may yell at him. If the shooter takes his eyes off the target, he usually blows the setup. Once a player has decided he has a good shot he must definitely begin to concentrate on the target he has picked out.

It has been tested and proved that peak concentration can be held only for a split second. Peak concentration should be reached at the exact moment at which the ball is released. When the fundamentals of shooting have been mastered to the point where proper shooting is automatic, players should start working to develop peak concentration as part of the daily practice sessions. Before practice and before a game, players should stare at the target so there is a familiar mental image of it in their minds when the time comes for a shot. There are six points which I consider the most important for players to concentrate on under game conditions:

1. Be sure that before a shot is taken there is good floor position and enough time to take a high-percentage shot.
2. Concentrate on the fundamentals of good shooting.

3. Have a target that is familiar and know how to use it.

4. Concentrate on having all shots split the middle of the basket but especially the first few shots of the game. This is important because it helps to build shooting confidence—players who miss their first shots often lose so much confidence that they may not hit during the entire game.

5. Be fully aware of where every shot hits in relation to the target.

6. Know how to adjust your shooting techniques to the target—don't just keep on missing the target in the same area and in the same way. For instance, if a shooter is missing to one side, he should move his target accordingly; more arm extension and a complete follow-through will help. If he is hitting short, he should move his target back. If he is hitting long, he should use the same target but give the ball a little higher arc; this will make the ball fall a bit shorter.

3

BASKETBALL'S BASIC

FIVE SHOTS

There are five fundamental shots in basketball:

1. Lay-up shot
2. Jump shot
3. One-hand set shot
4. Two-hand set shot
5. Hook shot

The proper technique of executing each of these will be presented in this chapter. Each technique assumes all of the interrelated fundamentals which we have discussed in the preceding chapter. Certain of these fundamentals are necessarily modified to fit a particular technique. Footwork, for example, is different for each shot, but concentration is a constant.

The Lay-Up Shot

The lay-up is used for shooting close to the basket, usually after a drive or on the tail of a fast-break situation. As its name implies, the shooter "lays" the ball up against the backboard a few inches above the rim so that it caroms down through the net. It is basketball's simplest shot, but it is often missed, usually during the crucial situation. Such misses usually result from the failure to observe the fundamentals, particularly a lack of concentration.

Two basic types of lay-up shots

The two basic types of lay-up shots are the underarm lay-up and the extended arm lay-up.

In the underarm technique, the shooter lays the ball against the backboard, with the back of his hand facing away from his body; in the extended arm lay-up, the ball is brought to a position above the head, with the back of the hand facing the shooter, and the ball is "pushed" to the basket (see Figure 3-1).

For certain situations the extended arm lay-up has an advantage over the underarm lay-up. For instance, a player in close to the basket and not moving very quickly uses the extended arm to supply needed extra power to the shot. Also, young beginners not too strong physically may need the extra strength which is inherent in this technique to get the ball to the basket. The little league and biddy players would be wise to use the extended arm push lay-up.

For shooting a lay-up at full speed I strongly advocate using the underarm technique. Of course, if a player has confidence in and success with the extended arm lay-up even at full speed, it would be unwise to change him. But for most boys approaching the basket at top speed, the extended arm lay-up may easily add too much speed to the flight of the ball. The underarm lay-up is designed to help a shooter ease up on a shot and release the ball softly (see Figure 3-2).

LAY UP SHOT

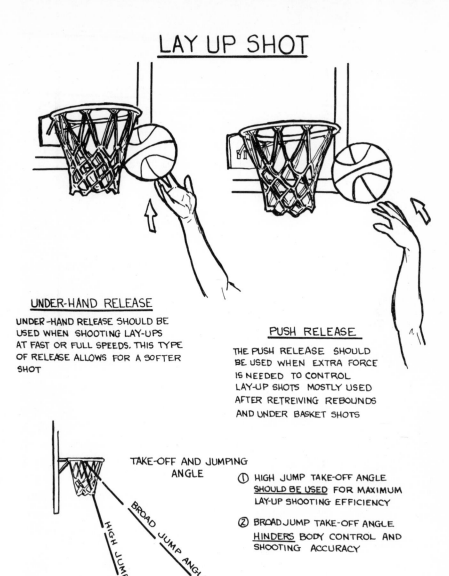

UNDER-HAND RELEASE

UNDER-HAND RELEASE SHOULD BE
USED WHEN SHOOTING LAY-UPS
AT FAST OR FULL SPEEDS. THIS TYPE
OF RELEASE ALLOWS FOR A SOFTER
SHOT

PUSH RELEASE

THE PUSH RELEASE SHOULD
BE USED WHEN EXTRA FORCE
IS NEEDED TO CONTROL
LAY-UP SHOTS MOSTLY USED
AFTER RETREIVING REBOUNDS
AND UNDER BASKET SHOTS

TAKE-OFF AND JUMPING
ANGLE

① HIGH JUMP TAKE-OFF ANGLE
SHOULD BE USED FOR MAXIMUM
LAY-UP SHOOTING EFFICIENCY

② BROAD JUMP TAKE-OFF ANGLE
HINDERS BODY CONTROL AND
SHOOTING ACCURACY

BROAD JUMP ANGLE

HIGH JUMP ANGLE

Diann

① CORRECT   ② INCORRECT

Fig. 3-1

Fig. 3-2: Bob Pettit completes an underarm lay-up at full speed.

Outstanding players of high school age or older can probably develop lay-up shots to a very high degree, but the coach must demand proficiency with each method.

Mechanics of the lay-up shot

FOOTWORK. To execute the lay-up properly the player must develop the footwork that will allow him to travel at full speed to the basket without breaking stride. If he does break stride, the defensive player will gain position on him and hinder or block an otherwise easy lay-up. The player should jump off the inside foot, so he should plant the inside foot close to the basket. He should have the feeling that he is high-jumping, not broad-jumping, to the basket.

Beginners usually have difficulty in mastering the correct footwork. I have found several drills effective for quickly developing this skill. First, have the beginner shoot the lay-up *without a ball* This drill enables him to concentrate solely on his footwork. Next, give him a basketball and have him shoot the lay-up after taking *one step* on to the inside foot. Then, have him take *three steps without dribbling* and shoot, jumping off the inside foot. For the fourth drill, have the shooter take *one* dribble and plant his inside foot in the desired take-off position near the basket. Repeat this 10 to 15 times, then have him complete the drill by shooting.

Let me re-emphasize that the take-off should be made close enough to the basket so that the shooter is jumping up rather than floating through the air— high-jumping rather than broad-jumping the shot. Broad-jumping the shot makes it more difficult and leads to numerous charging fouls and missed shots.

BODY BALANCE AND CONTROL. Good body balance and control are vital for the lay-up shooter. Traveling at top speed and shooting from close under the basket, he is quite apt to make body contact with the defense. As a player develops proper footwork and take-off position, he must learn to bend his knees enough to maintain body control and to get maximum height on his jump to the basket. He must also maintain body balance when alighting on the floor after shooting the lay-up lest he charge into opponents. Good balance will enable him to get back quickly on defense whether the shot is successful or not.

POSITION ON THE BALL. The shooter should hold the ball in a comfortable position close to the side of his body away from the defensive player. If the ball is held away from the body before and during the take-off, the player's center of gravity will be altered and he will be off balance. Also, control of the ball is hindered because the summation of forces will be broken. There is no body momentum behind the shot, the arm becomes tight and tense, and the player may feel a lack of strength. A shot under those conditions usually is short of its target. But if the ball is held close to the body before the jump, the player is free to extend his arm in the smooth, rhythmic, upward motion.

SIGHTING AND RELEASING BALL ON TARGET. The player must be as much aware of the defensive man as he is of the target. Most lay-ups are missed because the defensive man, by word or motion, disturbs the shooter. Usually the shooter will sight the target, but before he actually releases the ball, he glances at the defensive player. This interrupts his concentration on the target, so necessary at the exact moment of release.

The drill often used to combat this failing involves having a defensive player follow the shooter in for all lay-ups. We instruct the defensive man to have his inside arm up and to make some slight contact with the shooter's body. This gives the shooter practice in concentrating on the target regardless of contact or other distractions encountered in game conditions. If he approaches the basket from either side, he should use the backboard as a target. If he drives straight in, he should lay the ball over the front rim.

The ball should be held in the fingers of both hands as the player prepares to jump to the basket. To shoot the underhand lay-up, the shooting hand should move under the ball as the player starts to go upward. The other hand will stay on the ball until the shooting hand takes complete control of the shot. The ball should roll off the fingertips with good backspin. Even though the shooter is traveling at top speed, the upward movement of his arm will add extra speed to the flight of the ball. Usually a slight sidespin is given by turning the wrist on release. This will create a soft shot that will spin the ball in the basket, not bounce it straight back off the backboard, as so often happens when shooting is done at full speed.

For shooting the extended-arm or push lay-up shot, the ball is brought to a position just above the head on the take-off. The back of the shooting hand faces the shooter; the other hand is under the ball for control. At the top of his jump, the shooter pushes the ball to the basket with a forward push of the forearm and complete wrist follow-through similar to that of the one-hand set shot.

The Jump Shot

The jump shot is the most effective and potent shot in basketball today. A player who can jump quickly and who has the ability and skill to sink a 15- to 20-foot shot while in the air has developed a weapon that is almost impossible to stop. Unless the defensive player has the size, quickness, and tremendous reflexes of a Bill Russell, he stands little chance of blocking or even hindering this shot. I have seen Jerry West, who plays for the Los Angeles *Lakers*, score hundreds of points off his opponents, even when the defensive men had perfect position (see Figure 3-3). Jerry will either give

Fig. 3-3: In spite of K. C. Jones's perfect position, Jerry West gets his shot off. Note the flawless form in this jump shot.

a head fake or a hesitation, then jump high for the shot.
Of course he mixes this up with his drives and other
maneuvers which have made him one of the all-time
stars of the game. However, without his most effective
weapon, the jump shot, I feel he (and many other
players in the game today) would be greatly handi-
capped.

About the only thing the average defensive player
can do to stop the jump shot is to guess when to go up
with the shooter. Thus, having to anticipate the shot
before it actually begins leaves him wide open for defensive mistakes and errors. Probably the best tactic is
to force the offensive man out of position before he
receives the ball, or keep him from dribbling into
range, the perimeter from where he hits a good percentage of his attempted shots. If the offensive man
does get by, the next best defense is to distract the
shooter—faking him before he fakes you out of position or starts the shot. Such methods as jabbing at the
ball and retreating immediately, yelling, talking, or any
other action that will hinder the shooter's concentration is effective. If that doesn't work, jump at him with
at least one hand up around his eyes. Try to make him
flinch—bother his vision while he's sighting the target.

I point out some of these defensive fakes and maneuvers to stress the difficulties of trying to stop this
important shot. There are many reasons given why
shooters in basketball today are much better scorers
than a few years back. Better coaching, improved
equipment, rule changes, improved methods of employing the fast break, and so on, are all major factors, but
I feel sure most coaches will agree that the development and utilization of the jump shot has been the
greatest factor for the increase in scoring. It has left the
defensive man a great burden. Today there is much
greater effort being made on defense than ever before,
but the offense and especially the jump shot has over-
taken the old methods of playing defense. I urge all

young players and coaches to work hard at learning and developing the fundamentals and basic skills of the jump shot.

Mechanics of the jump shot

FOOTWORK AND BODY BALANCE. It is necessary to develop footwork and body balance for shooting the jump shot in three situations:

1. From a stationary position
2. After a dribble
3. After cutting to receive a pass

The basic technique for shooting the jump shot is the same in all of these situations; however, footwork and body balance may vary with each. The most important points to be emphasized when teaching jump-shooting in each of these situations are *maintenance of body balance* and *achievement of the very strongest and most comfortable jumping position.* I have found that the strongest jumping position is with the feet approximately shoulders' width apart and aligned almost parallel to the direction the player is facing. The knees must be bent and the weight distributed evenly if body balance is to be achieved.

STATIONARY POSITION. When the offensive player can maneuver his defensive man in close enough to receive the ball within good shooting range, he has gained a tremendous advantage. Now he will have the threat of his dribble to enable him to fake the shot and drive, or vice versa. The first thing the shooter should do after receiving the ball is to face the basket. This gives the shooter his maximum scoring threat and keeps the defensive man from overplaying or crowding him. The prime object of the shooter is to set himself up in a good shooting position. This is achieved by good footwork—bring the feet to approximately shoulders' width apart and almost parallel with the direction the shooter is facing. Most players prefer the foot on the side of the shooting hand to be slightly advanced.

I believe Tommy Heinsohn, a leading scorer for the Boston *Celtics* since 1956, has developed this stationary jump shot, along with his various fakes and drives, better than any player I know. Tommy has worked on this series of moves to the point where he is a tremendous threat from the stationary position. He can take the jump shot, pass, or drive, depending on the defensive player's position and the situation that develops during the game.

CUTTING TO RECEIVE THE PASS FOR THE JUMP SHOT. When teaching the technique for shooting the jump shot after a fast cut to receive the ball, the point to emphasize is *control of the center of gravity*. Perfect balance and body control are very important. Usually the younger or beginning player will have a tendency to be top-heavy, with his center of gravity too high and out of control. Another common fault—found even in the more advanced players—is the tendency to glide sideways in the direction of the cut after starting the jump. It is important to brake the cut and to take the shot while jumping straight up if maximum shooting efficiency is to be attained (see Figure 3-4, next page).

Good balance for the jump shot is obtained by proper footwork and the correct amount of bending of the knees. Taller boys especially often have difficulty running with their knees bent enough to achieve maximum body control, so this should be stressed constantly, particularly when they are cutting to receive a pass.

After receiving the ball the player must "square off" to the basket, turning his shoulders and feet toward it. This presents no problem if the player is cutting straight for the basket; however, if he is cutting laterally, it will be necessary for him to pivot on his *inside* foot, then bring his outside foot around into

JUMP SHOT

INCORRECT
A LATERAL JUMP WILL HINDER MAXIMUM SHOOTING EFFICIENCY

CORRECT
FOR MAXIMUM EFFICIENCY, A PLAYER SHOULD JUMP STRAIGHT UP IN LINE WITH THE BASKET

INCORRECT
A LATERAL JUMP WILL CREATE A VERY DIFFICULT OFF-BALANCE SHOT

Diann

Fig. 3-4

proper position. Proper footwork here does not come automatically; it must be practiced regularly along with the other skills.

JUMP SHOT AFTER THE DRIBBLE. This is the most common maneuver used when shooting the jump shot. Again, proper footwork must be used to achieve body balance. The footwork for the jump shot off the dribble is very similar to that for the jump shot after a cut. First, the player should be able to maneuver with the dribble close enough to obtain a high percentage shot. When he reaches this area, he brakes his drive by planting his *inside* or *leading foot* and quickly "squares off" into the correct jumping position *facing* the basket. The correct footwork should enable the player to take the shot by jumping straight up from a balanced position. A tip to aid the player in maintaining body balance and control: have him become conscious of keeping his head directly above an imaginary line drawn between his feet. If his head is in front or behind this line he will be off balance.

One of the most common errors made in shooting the jump shot off the dribble is rushing the shot. This can be prevented if the player will bring the ball into the proper starting position before beginning the shot. The rushed or jerky shot impairs the rhythmic flow that goes with a smooth summation-of-forces shot.

POSITION OF THE BALL. The ball should be brought relatively close to the body to coordinate the beginning of the shot before the player starts his upward jump. It should be held somewhere between the shoulders and the eyes, depending on how close to the basket he is and how strong his defensive player is. If the shooter is in close to the basket he doesn't need much force to control the shot, so he can hold the ball at a higher position, even a little higher than his head. This will enable him to release the ball quicker; it also makes it harder for the defensive man to block or hinder the shot. However, if the shooter is located farther out on

the court, he will need the extra force furnished by a
complete extension of the arm. In this case the ball
should be started lower, some place close to shoulder
level. This shot takes a little longer to execute and
release because the player is at a greater distance from
the basket. He should not take the shot unless he has
time to line himself up for a smooth, rhythmic shot.
This shot is controlled mostly by the extension of the
arm—the elbow creates a leverage, and the wrist follows through. The over-the-head jump shot leverage is
controlled mainly by wrist snap.

SIGHTING AND RELEASING BALL ON TARGET. One of the
most crucial points to teach is to ensure that the
player releases the ball at the very peak of the jump
(see Figure 3-5). If the player shoots on the way up
(too early) or releases the ball on his downward movement (too late), he does not have the necessary body
rhythm and coordination to execute the shot correctly.
A slight hesitation should be employed at the very
peak just before shooting the ball. This split second
will help the shooter line up the target and will allow
all the body's momentum—built up as the summation
of forces—to catch up and be utilized at the exact
moment of release.

Don't wait until reaching the top of the jump to
line up the direction and sight on the target area—do
it on the way up. This must be done, however, with the
awareness of reaching peak concentration at the final
release and follow-through.

Different techniques and
jumping positions

The jump shot as we know it today got started as a
tremendous scoring weapon right after World War II.
Since then it has evolved into many different styles and
techniques. In this chapter, I have been referring to the
method employed by most players and coaches—that in

JUMP SHOT

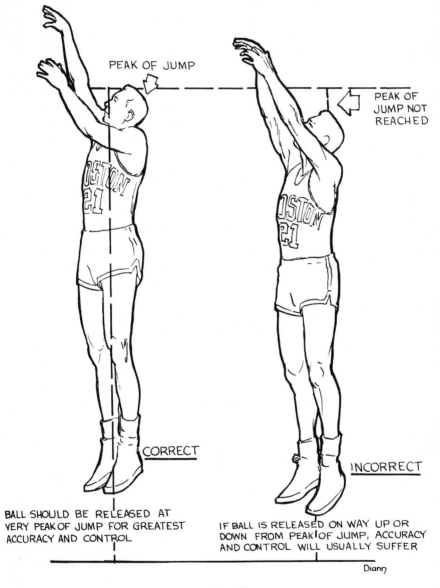

PEAK OF JUMP

PEAK OF JUMP NOT REACHED

CORRECT

INCORRECT

BALL SHOULD BE RELEASED AT VERY PEAK OF JUMP FOR GREATEST ACCURACY AND CONTROL

IF BALL IS RELEASED ON WAY UP OR DOWN FROM PEAK OF JUMP, ACCURACY AND CONTROL WILL USUALLY SUFFER

Diann

Fig. 3-5

which the shooter jumps straight up with a maximum leap, ideal for use behind a screen or pick. I mention this because there is some controversy over which method is the best or easiest. Many coaches say it is more comfortable and easier to shoot with a lesser jump—in which the shooter's feet barely leave the floor. Bob Cousy used to tell me that this was the way he preferred to shoot the jump shot, but he qualified that by adding that he didn't use it behind screens because he needed a higher jump to obtain a clear view of the basket and target. A great dribbler and driver, Cousy used the low jump when he could drive around completely clear of the defensive man. But he agreed that it probably was not as effective in most situations where the defense was playing tight. He developed this shot to the point where he felt more comfortable using it than the method of crouching lower and going up with a maximum jump, such as Jerry West or Oscar Robertson might do (see Figure 3-6). Cousy's feet are together when he leaves the ground. He has mentioned that this type of jump shot is executed much like a long, one-hand set shot in which the feet must leave the floor to generate enough power to control the shot.

Another very effective style—one becoming more popular every day—is the fade-away jump shot. This is probably the most difficult shot to learn—and teach— but it is also the most difficult to defend against. I strongly advise that young players avoid the fade-away until they completely master the regular straight-up jump shot. If a boy does not understand and is not able to execute the regular jump shot, the fader will only confuse him and certainly cut down on his efficiency. Professional players are about the only ones with enough experience and ability to use it consistently. Paul Arizin, who played for the Philadelphia Warriors and was an all-league player for many years, was probably the first, and one of the most successful players, to use it. Arizin was only 6′ 4″ tall, which is

Fig. 3-6: Here is the jump shot *par excellence*. Oscar Robertson illustrates every fundamental mentioned in this section.

considered very short by professional league standards. However, because of his ability to stop quickly, fake his defensive man and employ the fade-away jumper, he was able to shoot and score against great defensive players who were much taller and sometimes quicker than he. Mainly because of this one shot, Paul was the leading scorer in the N.B.A. for many years. He used to stress one important point when teaching the fade-away jump shot: fade in a *direct line away* from the basket while in the air. Never fade to one side or in a lateral angle to the basket—if this happens, the shooter has to judge the distance to the basket and also know how much he has to compensate for his lateral movement while in the air. If the shooter fades back in a straight line from the basket, he does not have the tendency to shoot wide, and he need concentrate only on judging the distance to his target.

The One-Hand Set Shot

The one-hand set shot was first made popular by the great Hank Luisetti, who played for Stanford University in the mid-1930s. Until that time the two-hand set shot had been considered the only reliable and acceptable shot. The majority of coaches frowned on any one-handed attempts at the basket, except lay-ups, feeling that any outside shooting not done with two hands was unorthodox and bad percentage shooting. Then along came Luisetti. With ceaseless dedication to the game, he developed the one-hand set. At first he had tremendous success on the West Coast using and scoring with his new-found weapon, but he had few believers until his team traveled East. On that trip he scored over 50 points in one game—unheard of in that era. This aroused the curiosity and interest of most coaches. Many decided to spend more time and research on this new shot, to see if there really were some advantages to it that were being overlooked.

It didn't take the coaches and players long to discover it could offer many favorable improvements to their game. They found they could release the ball quicker, and do so from many positions that were unsuited to the two-hander. This created new problems for the defensive players—now they had to be wary of new fakes and maneuvers, and had to play their men much closer. It also popularized the running one-hand shot, which was seldom used prior to that time and was the forerunner to the one-hand jump shot.

Many people have said that the development of the one-hand shot has been the greatest improvement in offense that the game has ever experienced. Although the jump shot is still considered the most effective shot today, it is actually just the old one-hander executed in a different manner and position.

Everyone will agree that a player should use his strongest and most successful shot on the free-throw line. There is no defensive man to worry about and enough time (10 seconds) to concentrate completely on the necessary elements to make the shot good, hence there is no reason to use any other shot but the most successful. Most coaches and players use and recommend the one-hand set shot for shooting free throws, and it follows, I feel, that it is also the most generally successful and reliable shot available for all situations—given enough time to make it.

Mechanics of the
one-hand set shot

The one-hand set shot was used as a model for discussing the interrelated fundamentals of shooting in Chapter 2, and the fundamentals for executing it have thus already been presented. The following brief summary of the basic mechanics of the shot is offered to better explain it and its relationship to other shots under discussion.

ONE HAND SET SHOT

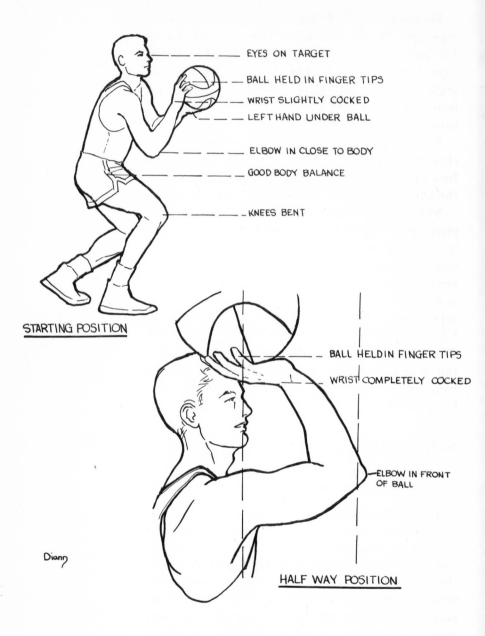

EYES ON TARGET

BALL HELD IN FINGER TIPS

WRIST SLIGHTLY COCKED

LEFT HAND UNDER BALL

ELBOW IN CLOSE TO BODY

GOOD BODY BALANCE

KNEES BENT

STARTING POSITION

BALL HELD IN FINGER TIPS

WRIST COMPLETELY COCKED

ELBOW IN FRONT OF BALL

HALF WAY POSITION

Diann

Fig. 3-7

FOOTWORK AND BODY BALANCE. The feet should be approximately shoulders' width apart, the right foot a few inches in advance of the left. The toe of the right foot should be pointed at a 30- to 45-degree angle to the target. Knees should be comfortably bent and the weight evenly distributed for proper balance.

POSITION OF THE BALL. The ball should be held close to the body, approximately shoulder high. The back of the right hand should be facing the shooter; the left hand is placed under the ball for control.

SIGHTING AND RELEASING BALL ON TARGET. The player must begin his concentration on the target area prior to beginning the shot. The shot is begun with a lifting of the elbow followed by a forward push of the forearm. The legs are straightened to give extra power to the shot, the amount of extension depending on the distance of the shot. A complete follow-through of the wrist completes the release. The eyes should remain on the target area after the ball is in its trajectory toward the basket. Figure 3-7 pinpoints the important fundamentals of the one-hand set shot.

The Two-Hand Set Shot

Adolph Rupp's "Theory"

The one-hander is probably the most widely used shot ever developed, and it is considered the most effective in basketball today. However, there are still many players and coaches who use the two-hand set shot diligently and to great advantage. Probably the most obvious usage of the two-hand set is as a long-range outside shot, one that is always hard to guard against if the shooter is skilled enough to hit with a high degree of accuracy. It can be applied effectively at the greater distances where all one-handers lose their effectiveness.

Adolph Rupp, the great coach at the University of Kentucky, who has developed so many national championship teams, makes the long two-hander the backbone of his offensive shooting. He works hard with his players to develop their ability to use this basic shot. He theorizes that if they can hit the long shots they will have a much easier time getting and sinking the short ones. If the long shots are going in, this will bring the defense out, opening up the inside plays and patterns. He points out that most defenses today sag in the middle, since few players are able to shoot the long shot with a good percentage. Therefore, he spends more time on the two-hand set than most coaches, who today emphasize the shorter shots. Rupp also advocates that the long shot be used mainly by the guards. He has achieved great success, and I believe his technique and theory deserves much consideration.

Other advantages
of two hands

This shot offers a second big advantage: it puts the shooter in a good, strong position to pass, shoot, or drive. Compared with the one-hand set shot, in which the feet are spaced farther apart, the two-hand set enables the shooter to take the first step much quicker, which will discourage the defensive man from guarding him too tightly.

I strongly urge that younger players and most beginners—who need extra strength and power to get the ball to the basket with good accuracy—start with the two-hand set shot. Many smaller boys develop bad habits early because they have to *throw* the ball to the basket. They cannot shoot it with the proper fundamentals because they do not have the necessary strength to do so. A bad habit takes many long hours of practice to correct, and sometimes can handicap a player's style and efficiency permanently. With maturity and strength, the player can switch over to the one-handed techniques and more advanced styles of shooting.

Mechanics of the two-hand set shot

FOOTWORK AND BODY BALANCE. For the two-hand shot, two distinct styles of footwork and body position have been developed.

One style, preferred in the East, places the feet together before the ball is released. It is claimed that this stance gets a little more body and leg effort into the shot, making it easier to get the ball to the basket with less effort and more control. It is also claimed that it is easier to give a higher arc to the trajectory of the shot, an advantage in getting the ball over a defensive player's outstretched arms.

The other style places the left foot slightly forward. This stance, it is claimed, gives the shooter a more comfortable feeling as well as a stronger, steadier position from which to shoot, pass, or drive. Today, most styles of play stress the running and driving offenses, and I feel the latter position offers more advantages. However, the basic point to strive for is balance, and a player should be encouraged to use the style of footwork that suits him best. Comfort, too, is important in all shooting; this can be improved by certain positions of the feet. As in other shots, the degree of knee bend depends on the distance the shot is attempted from the basket.

Bob Davies vs. Bobby Wanzer

A digression regarding these two styles of shooting the two-hand set shot involves two great guards of the early 1950s: Bob Davies and Bobby Wanzer. Both attended Seton Hall University in their college days. When the N.B.A. was started after World War II, both boys wound up playing for the Rochester *Royals* in the eastern division. Both were chosen for all-star and all-league teams for many years, and were for a long time considered the best back-court combination in basketball. They were the two leading scorers on the *Royals* team that won the N.B.A. world championship in the 1950-51 season. These two great players both depended on the two-hand set shot as their number one weapon and basic shot.

Bobby Wanzer, considered by many the greatest shooter of that era, preferred to place his feet together, whereas Bob Davies, considered the best driver in the league, liked to place his left foot slightly in advance of his right.

POSITION OF THE BALL. The most commonly developed two-hand set shot is executed by starting the ball about chest high with the elbows in fairly close to the body in a relaxed, comfortable position. An unsteady sensation is created if the elbows are extended too far from the body. This is comparable to the golfer who holds his elbows too far from his body, cutting down on his accuracy and rhythm. But if the elbows are held in too tight, the shooter may become cramped and lose the freedom to make a natural, smooth shot. The ball is therefore held fairly close to the body—approximately 10-12 inches from the chest area.

The ball should be held with both hands, the fingers on the sides of the ball (the ball should *never* touch the palms). The fingers should be spread comfortably, the thumbs somewhat behind the ball and almost pointing toward each other. The ball should be gripped firmly but gently, as one might handle expensive china—in a relaxed manner but firmly enough to control and not drop or fumble. Good form is depicted in Figure 3-8.

TWO HAND SET SHOT

SET POSITION

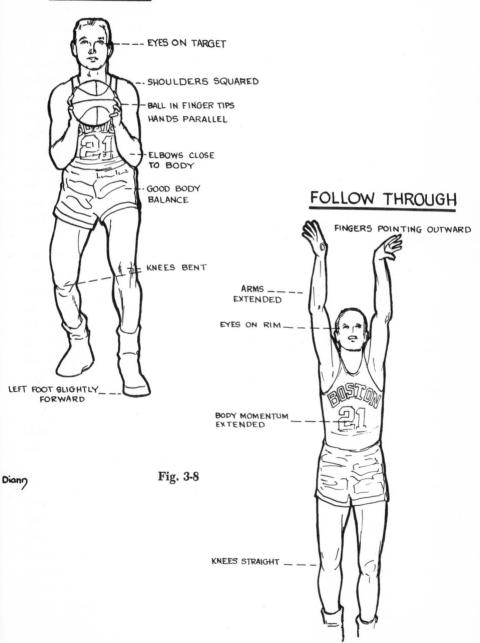

EYES ON TARGET

SHOULDERS SQUARED

BALL IN FINGER TIPS
HANDS PARALLEL

ELBOWS CLOSE
TO BODY

GOOD BODY
BALANCE

KNEES BENT

LEFT FOOT SLIGHTLY
FORWARD

FOLLOW THROUGH

FINGERS POINTING OUTWARD

ARMS
EXTENDED

EYES ON RIM

BODY MOMENTUM
EXTENDED

KNEES STRAIGHT

Diann

Fig. 3-8

SIGHTING AND RELEASING BALL ON TARGET. The shot is started in the usual (basic) way; that is, from the feet, which starts the generation of power up through the legs, body, and arm until the summation of forces reaches its peak as the ball is released. The target area is sighted over the ball prior to the forward thrust of the arms that sends the ball toward the basket. The ball should roll off the fingertips. A good backspin will result if the proper amount of wrist snap and fingertip control is applied. A good follow-through is important—both arms should be completely extended, with the fingers and wrist in a natural position.

Two-hand over-the-head set shot

In another style of shooting the two-hand set, the ball is held and started over the shooter's head. The arms are slightly bent in a relaxed manner, the elbows almost pointing at the basket. This method is difficult to master, mainly because the ball is released above the head and the shooter does not have the benefit of visually lining up the ball with the target area. However, it does offer some extremely important advantages:

1. It puts the defender at great disadvantage, for he has to play his man very closely if he is to hinder or block the shot. This leaves him vulnerable to quick maneuvers and fakes, and he may be caught off balance.

2. Since the ball is shot quicker and with a higher arc of trajectory, this is an ideal shot for shooting from behind and over screens. A quick shot and release can multiply into many advantages and points during the course of a game or a season.

3. It creates a natural position for the player to either shoot or pass, especially if he intends to pass

to the pivot man, because this is the easiest (and recommended) method of getting the ball into the pivot area. Therefore, it sets up an ideal situation of either faking a pass and shooting, or vice versa.

The essential disadvantages of this shot include the following:

1. Because the ball must travel a longer distance when it is started over the player's head, it takes a little longer to bring the ball down to the proper position before starting a dribble or drive.

2. The over-the-head shot does not receive the full benefit of the extension of the arms, as does the two-hand chest shot. It is, therefore, probably a little less effective at longer range. It requires that a little more force be generated by the legs and body—the additional knee bend thus required to shoot at the same distance will slightly delay the release.

3. Since the shooter is standing in a more erect position to make this shot, he has a tendency to place his feet closer together. This will hinder a quick start, for that stance is not the good, strong starting position required to push off for the all-important fast step when trying to beat or drive around the defensive man.

Considering all its advantages and disadvantages, I definitely feel that a boy who can achieve the same accuracy and efficiency with the over-the-head two-hand set shot will garner more benefits than with the two-hand chest set shot.

Three great
over-the-head shooters

There come to mind three great players who all relied on the over-the-head two-hand set and used it with great effectiveness.

Bones McKinney

Horace "Bones" McKinney was an All-American in college and a first-team, all-league player for Red Auerbach and the old Washington *Capitols* in the early days of the N.B.A. Bones is now head coach at Wake Forest College and one of the most respected and successful college coaches in the country. He was one of the first advocates of the over-the-head shot who enjoyed a signal success with it. During my first two years in professional ball I was fortunate enough to play with and under him as he served as a player-coach during the 1950–51 season. He had developed a series of moves while holding the ball directly over his head. From this position he could either shoot, pass, or drive with great deception, making him one of the finest competitors the game has ever known.

Carl Braun

A professional all-star and all-league player with the New York *Knickerbockers* for many years, Carl was considered one of the deadliest shooters in the league during his 15-year career. Although lacking any outstanding speed, he was very hard to guard against, for he held the ball very high above his head while shooting, and the defender had to anticipate the shot in order to try to stop it. Carl was a leading scorer for the *Knickerbockers* and one of the top scorers in the league for many years.

Larry Friend

Larry Friend became an All-American at the University of California while playing for Pete Newell in the late 1950s. He was the number one draft choice of the New York *Knickerbockers* after graduation. He played with them a full year, but hurt his knee and was forced to retire. Larry was one of the few who used and developed the over-the-head set shot. Two years after he left the *Knicks*, Abe Saperstein started the new A.B.L. basketball league that featured the three-point basket for any shot made beyond the 25-foot line. This inspired Larry to try a comeback, although his knee was still bothering him and had cut down his speed and maneuverability a great deal. While playing for me with the Los Angeles *Jets*, Larry became the leading three-point scorer in the league, a very valuable player, mainly because of this one shot that he had developed to the highest degree.

The Hook Shot

The hook shot is probably the most difficult of all shots to block or defend against, and is probably the most difficult of all shots to execute with a high degree of proficiency. Because the ball is held so far away from the body and there is so little opportunity for visual lineup with the basket, it is controlled and released more by feel than by aim, unlike most other shots. It is primarily designed for use by the big centers and pivot men, but has been developed and used by many guards and forwards.

Guard Position

Bob Cousy was one of the first and is undoubtedly the most famous guard ever to use this shot consistently in top competition. Because of his small size, compared with most professionals, he found he would have many of his lay-ups and easy short shots blocked by the bigger men who usually congest the key area. Therefore, he practiced many long and tedious hours developing his hook shot with both left and right hands. One of his favorite and most effective maneuvers was to lead the fast break. If no one was in the clear, he would drive by his man and take the running hook anywhere from five to 15 feet from the basket on either side. But this is absolutely one of the toughest shots in basketball, and certainly not recommended for the beginner, or even the average player. I feel that only the very outstanding drivers and shooters should try to use it from the guard position.

Forward Position

Many forwards have had outstanding success with the hook, when driving toward the middle and releasing the ball somewhere in the area of the key. It is a special skill of such players as Elgin Baylor of the *Lakers*, Cliff Hagan of the *Hawks*, and Tom Heinsohn of the *Celtics* (see Figure 3-9), and the defense goes crazy trying to stop it.

I definitely feel that younger boys learning to play forward should experiment with this shot and the series of fakes and maneuvers that go with it. If they can develop it, it will be an invaluable weapon in their offensive game and will set up some of their other shots and fakes.

Pivot Position

There is no doubt that the hook shot is one of the most valuable and productive weapons the pivot man can use. Most of the great offensive centers have developed the hook shot to almost a science. Many can turn and shoot before sighting the basket, just because they know where they are on the floor before firing the shot. Of course, they will glance at the rim and target area just before releasing the ball to achieve the highest degree of accuracy.

Among the greatest hook shooters have been George Mikan, in 1950 voted the greatest player for the half century by the A.P. sportswriters of America, and Bob Houbregs, the great All-American from the University of Washington. Bob became an outstanding professional player who shattered numerous scor-

Fig. 3-9: Tommy Heinsohn executes his version of the running hook. As you can see it's impossible to stop.

ing records before injuring his back and retiring at an early age. One of the greatest shooters in the game today is Bill McGill, playing for the Los Angeles *Lakers*. Many people say he has the deadliest hook shot in pro ball. He ranked as the highest-scoring player in the nation while playing for Jack Gardner at the University of Utah during the 1961-62 season. I strongly recommend that all young prospective basketball players who feel they will be big enough to play the center position work very hard to develop the hook shot to the best of their ability.

Mechanics of the
hook shot

FOOTWORK AND BODY BALANCE. As always, the key to all well-executed shots is good balance, obtained by proper footwork and stance. This is especially true for the hook shot because the player usually has to take a step and pivot before releasing the ball. The fact that he is in motion and holding the ball behind his body creates a handicap to aiming. All told, the hook is a very difficult shot even if all the other basic fundamentals are carried out well. In this shot, I particularly stress the importance of good balance which comes with the feet being used in the correct way.

The shooter usually receives the ball with his back to the basket. His feet should be lined up almost parallel and as far apart as the width of his shoulders, a stance that will give him a good strong jumping or reacting position if he has to reach for a bad pass. A fake with the head and shoulders usually precedes the long step and pivot before shooting. When he starts his pivot step the player should duck his inside shoulder and plant his inside foot firmly by bending his knee to gain good body balance and control. He should now be in the proper position to start his

HOOK SHOT

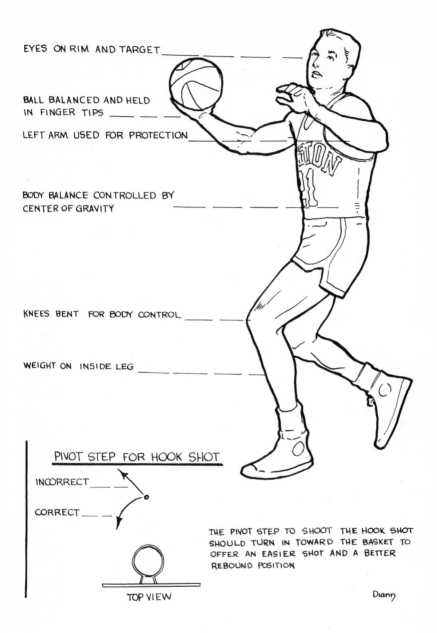

EYES ON RIM AND TARGET

BALL BALANCED AND HELD
IN FINGER TIPS

LEFT ARM USED FOR PROTECTION

BODY BALANCE CONTROLLED BY
CENTER OF GRAVITY

KNEES BENT FOR BODY CONTROL

WEIGHT ON INSIDE LEG

PIVOT STEP FOR HOOK SHOT

INCORRECT

CORRECT

THE PIVOT STEP TO SHOOT THE HOOK SHOT
SHOULD TURN IN TOWARD THE BASKET TO
OFFER AN EASIER SHOT AND A BETTER
REBOUND POSITION

TOP VIEW

Diann

Fig. 3-10

shot. There are, of course, various methods and techniques of shooting the hook shot; the form is not standardized as are most of the other basic shots. Many centers, for instance, will step away from the basket before releasing; others will step to one side toward the goal. Most coaches will stress the importance of stepping in the direction of the basket in order to be in good rebounding position if the shot is missed. I agree with this, and feel it is important to teach this strategy.

POSITION OF THE BALL. After catching the ball it should be held in a comfortable position, approximately waist high, and brought slightly toward the body before taking the long pivot step. This will help achieve quickness along with better balance.

As the step is started, the arms are fully extended, and will begin to move upward in a very smooth, rhythmic, sweeping motion. Both hands should remain on the ball until the shooting hand moves under the ball and takes over completely. The inside arm should continue to move up into a position that will help protect the ball from the defender (see Figure 3-10, page 79).

SIGHTING AND RELEASING BALL ON TARGET. Most hook shots are taken from the side and are aimed at the backboard as in the lay-up shot. Therefore, the target area must be the spot on the backboard at which the ball is to be shot. Sighting of this target area must come as soon as possible after the initial step, for the shot and peak concentration must be reached as the ball is released.

As always, the ball should be held in the fingers, not the palms of the hands. After the arm almost reaches its highest position, the release is guided by the wrist and fingertips. The ball will roll off the fingertips in a backward motion, giving the necessary backspin for a soft shot. At the last instant before the ball completely leaves the fingers, the wrist should be snapped to encourage the proper release.

Because the hook shot employs an almost complete sweep of the arm and takes a little longer to complete than most other shots, smooth, rhythmic motion should be stressed at all times. Any hurried, jerky shot will throw off accuracy and control. Remember that because the shooting hand is almost completely under the ball it is necessary to loft the ball in a little higher arc than for most shots, especially if the shot is taken from in front of the basket and the backboard is not used.

4

"FOUL! SHOOT ONE!"

I am sure every basketball player, coach and fan has had nightmares about the missed free throw that cost his team a valuable victory. Free-throw shooting is directly responsible, as well, for many extra wins during a season, and many coaches feel rightly that it is the most important factor in winning any close game.

All coaches should emphasize that free-throw shooting can be improved more than any other phase of shooting: it is the only exactly similar shot each player will have more than once (even a lay-up shot can be made in different ways); 10 seconds are allowed to prepare for and execute the shot, and the same conditions of distance and position on the court exist every time.

I urge that every boy be coached conscientiously on the fundamentals of the free-throw technique. Then, with determination and desire, and working on his own time, he can develop this very important basketball weapon. The shot is truly a feat of muscle-memory and repetition. I like to compare it to a person giving a speech: the more he practices, the better his delivery will be. The same applies to shooting free throws. The more it is practiced, the better it becomes; the player's muscles will retain the same method and degree of success in a game that they acquired in practice. There is no substitute for hard work and desire in any sport.

History of Free Throws

In the early history of basketball, all free throws were taken by the same player each time a foul was committed. This was somewhat analogous to football where each team has a kicking specialist whose job is to boot in the extra points after a touchdown.

In the 1920s, however, the rule was changed: the player fouled had to shoot his own free throw. This new rule changed the entire complexion of the game—especially for the coaches who now had to make sure that each player learned and developed a successful free throw. Without this skill, a team is at a tremendous disadvantage.

Then, in the 1930s, the rule was changed again to allow the player and the team to decide whether to shoot the free throw or take the ball out of bounds and retain possession. However, this created problems in the later parts of a game, and certainly was a big advantage for the team that was ahead. It encouraged stalling, and made it almost impossible for the team behind to get possession of the ball. Because it greatly hindered continuity and scoring, the rule was changed shortly afterward; now the player fouled has to shoot the free throw.

Another important rule, adopted in the early 1940s, allowed one offensive and one defensive player to line up beneath the basket on each side of the free-throw line. This gave another extreme advantage to the team with a big, tall, strong rebounder. Now the shooter would sometimes "miss" on purpose, directing the ball to the side where his tall teammate was lined up, allowing him to tip in for two points instead of the one-point free throw. Later, this rule was changed. Now only the defensive players can line up on the inside of the basket on both sides of the free-throw line.

Some minor rule changes were made during the 1950s, such as the one-and-one foul shot. At one time, a player who missed his first attempt when a bonus foul was called was automatically given another try. This still applies in the bonus situation in professional basketball. However, it is exactly the opposite in college and high school basketball, in which the player is rewarded with another try only if he succeeds in his first. The effect of this rule has been to encourage the player to practice and improve his free-throw shooting. On the other hand, the rule that gives the shooter an extra free throw when he misses the first seems to encourage lack of concentration.

Regardless of the year or the rule, free throws have always played a vital part in basketball. It is very hard indeed to have a consistently winning team unless the players are good free-throw shooters.

Why I Sought Perfection

Although I always felt I was a little above average in the ability to shoot free throws in high school and in my first two years at college, it wasn't until my junior year at USC that I really felt a sense of pride and dedication in improving this skill to the very highest degree possible.

I guess it's natural for a person to enjoy something he's fairly successful at. In my junior year I mixed in many hours of extra practice on the free-throw line, and went all 12 league games in our conference without missing a free throw. I wasn't that fortunate in our practice games, but I still managed to wind up second in the nation for free-throw shooting. My shooting percentage was around 87 per cent for the year, which included all games.

I'm sure this was the beginning of my desire to concentrate more than I had before. I was receiving a fair amount of publicity and acclaim regarding this part of my game. I could feel the pressure of the spectators every time I missed one. So I made up my mind to become as good as my natural ability would allow. Of course, no one ever knows for sure if or when he has reached his maximum potential. But I did practice and experiment, and analyzed the art of free-throw shooting as much as the busy schedule would allow during my years as an active player. And I hope some of my hints and suggestions will help some players and coaches over the rough road to success.

Looking back over my college years and games, I believe the greatest pressure I sensed at the free-throw line was in my junior year, when I went the 12 conference games without a miss. This had never been done before—nor has it been done since. The papers started writing about it during the middle of the season and had it built up to something pretty big as we were coming into the 12th and last game of the year against our old crosstown rival, UCLA. I shot only three free throws in that game, but each time the ball seemed to weigh 10 pounds and my knees felt as though they were turning to rubber. Luckily, each of the three shots went in, and that was the beginning of a free-throw reputation I always tried to live up to.

Many of the basketball writers and fans wondered aloud if I could do it two years in a row. . . . During the first league game of my senior year, I was feeling pretty confident after eight months of over-glorifying my record and my ability. Calmly I stepped up—and *missed* my first free throw of the season!

My Years in the Pros

After graduating from USC in 1950, I signed a bonus contract with the old Brooklyn *Dodgers* to play ball in their farm system. I also signed a professional basketball contract that year with the now-defunct *Capitols* of Washington, D.C. They folded in January of 1951, and the following year I was drafted by the Boston *Celtics*. I spent ten full seasons with the Boston team. During the time I spent in the N.B.A. as a player, I was fortunate enough to establish most of today's free-throw records. Some of these include: (1) the highest percentage for a career—.883 per cent, or 3143 free throws out of 3557 attempts; (2) the highest percentage for any one season (1958-59)—.932 per cent, or 342 free throws out of 367 attempts; (3) the highest percentage for play-off games (at least 50)—.911 per cent, or 370 free throws out of 406 attempts in 78 play-off games; (4) the most consecutive foul shots in one season— 55, made in the period Nov. 22, 1957 through Dec. 27, 1957; (5) the most consecutive free throws in one play-off series—56, made in the period March 18, 1959 through April 9, 1959; (6) the most official free-throw championships—seven.

Free-throw highlights

Some of the experiences which highlighted this period still make me laugh, although some still make me nervous. I remember my last season with the Boston *Celtics*. I was shooting better than 92 per cent from the free-throw line as we went into our last game of the season with the Syracuse *Nationals*.

However, the many injuries I suffered that season had caused me to miss a number of games, so I still needed ten more free-throw attempts to qualify for the free-throw championship. The Syracuse team was aware of this, and naturally they all were being very careful not to foul me. We had already won the division and league championships so Red Auerbach, our coach, instructed the players to get the ball to me as much as possible so that I might qualify for the free-throw championship. It finally got to the point where I would receive the ball and then start dribbling toward some of the Syracuse players, hoping for a chance to get fouled so I could shoot some free throws. Of course Syracuse didn't want me to win this title at their expense, so they were actually falling away from me to avoid any contact whatsoever. We finally called time out and decided that, since they were going to let me shoot, we would just run up as high a score as possible and try to embarrass them this way. After I had made a few easy baskets, Syracuse finally called time out and decided they should start playing their normal defense. When the game was over, I had shot 11 free throws. The first ten were successful, which gave me enough to win the free-throw championship for the seventh time. However, I missed my 11th attempt and still have the memory and regret of missing the last free throw during my ten and one-half years of regular competition in the N.B.A.

A real boner

Probably one of the most embarrassing moments in my career, especially at the free-throw line, occurred on national television. I was being interviewed by Marty Glickman during a half-time ceremony. I was trying to give hints and suggestions to the TV viewers and younger players on how to shoot free throws. After Marty had given me a tremendous build-up as "the greatest free-throw shooter in the history of the game," and had mentioned many of the records I held, he asked me to describe and demonstrate my technique. So I proceeded to describe how I did this and that, and how easy it was if only one followed these simple rules and techniques. Finally, Marty said, "Why don't you shoot a couple and show us how easy it is?" So I stepped up to the line —and naturally missed every time I tried. Bill Russell, who was standing close by, really broke up everyone when he hollered, "That's the same way you taught me to shoot free throws, Sharman!"

My tightest spot

I can still recall the greatest pressure shot I ever tried from the foul line. This occurred before Bill Russell had joined the Boston *Celtics*, when we were still looking for our first championship. It was the latter part of the 1952-53 season; the Rochester *Royals* were battling the *Lakers* for first place in the Western Division, and we were fighting for first place in the Eastern Division. This was a very crucial game for both teams and could possibly decide the outcome for first place in both divisions. We were playing in Rochester before a capacity house. Tension ran very high that night, and the game was very close and hard fought right down to the wire. Both coaches were using their time-outs to employ every possible strategy to take advantage of each situation. Finally, with five seconds remaining in the game and the score tied, Rochester took a shot and missed. The *Celtics* took an immediate time-out as soon as they got possession of the rebound. Both teams had now used up all their allowed time-outs. After the *Celtics* put the ball in play and missed the last shot, one of the Rochester players grabbed the rebound, and, forgetting that they didn't have any left, hollered "Time out!" to the nearest official as the gun went off.

Of course, as in most similar cases, this led to a long and heated discussion by the Rochester coach, Les Harrison. He argued—to officials, timers, scorers, and anyone else who would listen to him—that the gun had gone off before the time-out was called. Coach Auerbach had motioned to me immediately that I was to shoot the free throw; however, it was a good 10 or 15 minutes before order was finally restored. This lapse in time had served to bring the pressure to the point that I felt like someone strapped on an iron suit and it was almost impossible to bend my arms into the correct position.

To be honest, I really blew the shot by shooting too long. But fate was on my side this evening, for the ball hit the back rim very hard, bounced high in the air, banked off the backboard, hit the rim again, and finally settled into the basket. I am sure it was probably the most important and luckiest free throw I ever made.

Mikan's free-throw drama

I believe that one of the greatest clutch performances ever given at the free-throw line was the one by the incredible George Mikan in the 1954 All-Star game in Madison Square Garden. This game is still considered by many to be the greatest All-Star game ever played. It established an attendance record: 16,-487 spectators. It also is the only one that ever ended up in overtime—thanks to the greatness of Mikan, who sank two free throws after the game was over. It had been a thrill-packed game. Then, with three seconds left and the score tied, Bob Cousy scored a 20-foot shot, which everyone figured would be the winning basket. However, the West team threw the ball in bounds and called an immediate time-out. This gave them the ball out of bounds at center court with only two seconds remaining. The West had mapped out a quick play that would get the ball in deep to Mikan for the last shot. When Mikan received the inbounds pass, he quickly faked his defensive opponent out of position and was fouled, preventing an easy lay-up. As Mikan was fouled the gun went off to end the game. Now Mikan had to make both free throws to tie; if he missed either one, the East squad would win the game. The East team, realizing that he would be shooting under pressure, called time-out twice in a row in order to let the pressure mount. Approximately five minutes had ticked by before referee Sid Borgia finally gave the ball to Mikan.

The crowd roared as the great pro "with ice-water in his veins" sank the first toss. Then he leisurely walked away from the line, took a deep breath, returned, and took aim for the second try. The ball sank cleanly through the strings to force the annual All-Star game into overtime for the first and only time.

In the overtime Bob Cousy scored 10 points to clinch the victory for the Eastern All-Stars. It was truly an historic game, and it is still described as the greatest the annual classic has ever produced.

Greatest free-throw shooter of all time

Whenever free-throw shooting is discussed, the name of Bunny Levitt will almost always appear. Bunny is a great little guy who tours the world, teaching boys and girls his philosophy and the fundamentals of basketball. As a representative of the Converse Rubber Company, he puts on basketball clinics, lectures, demonstrations, and the like, whenever requested. His specialty is the free throw. Although Bunny, at five feet eight inches, was never big enough to play professional ball, he was an outstanding all-around player and ball handler for many teams. With years of practice and hard work, he developed the greatest free-throw record of all time. In a publicized competitive tournament, he made 499 consecutive free throws without a miss. Then he missed one, and went on to make 371 more consecutive shots. This is undoubtedly the greatest free-throw record of all time. It even appeared in Ripley's *Believe It Or Not.*

5

SINKING THE FREE THROW

The Five Foul-Line Shots

The following five shots are most often seen in foul shooting:

1. The one-hand set free throw
2. The two-hand underhand free throw
3. The two-hand chest free throw
4. The jump-shot free throw
5. The two-hand overhead free throw

Each of these free throws will be discussed; however, the fundamentals for each have been explained in previous chapters.

One of the most important points is that most outstanding players use the same shot on the free-throw line as they do on the long set shot. Because so many players shoot one-handed today, the most

common type of free-throw shot is the one-hand set;
however, at the free-throw line the player usually
uses the technique he is most proficient at.

One-hand set free throw

There is little doubt that the one-hand set shot is
the most common free-throw shot used today. Most
players shoot one-handed from any position on the
court. This is the method I have always used, and I
feel certain it offers more advantages than most
others. Players still undecided as to which technique
they will try to develop should seriously consider this
style.

Two-hand chest free throw

Probably the second most popular free throw today
is the two-hand chest shot. It was the most common
method by far about 20 or 30 years ago—or until the
great Hank Luisetti developed the one-hand set shot
and made it so popular.

Bobby Wanzer and Dolph Schayes both used the
two-hand chest free throw. They are the only two
players, besides myself, who have ever shot more
than 90 per cent from the free-throw line in the history of the N.B.A. (The 90 per cent mark for shooting free throws has often been compared to the .400
batting-average mark of baseball players.) Wanzer
was the first professional to tap this elusive figure,
which he did during the 1951-52 season while playing for the Rochester *Royals*. Since then, Dolph
Schayes has broken the mark twice, and I was fortunate enough to do it three times. My highest mark
—93.2 per cent—still stands as the N.B.A. free-throw
record.

Two-hand underhand
free throw

For many years the two-hand underhand free throw was used by nearly all the outstanding players, and was considered by many to be the only *correct* method. Of course, opinions change as the years pass; new shots and techniques were evolved. However, many coaches and players still use and teach this method. Wilt Chamberlain, unquestionably the greatest scorer in the history of the game, has always had difficulty in shooting free throws. He has experimented with many methods and styles, but finds the two-hand underhand shot the most successful for him. A few others in the N.B.A. also use this shot, but its popularity is on the wane.

From the coaching standpoint, the biggest advantage of the two-hand underhand free throw is its position on the line. The player's arms hang straight down in a very relaxed position (see Figure 5-1)—and it is in the arms that pressure and tension are felt most. Whenever the arms are tight, the follow-through on a normal shot is usually hampered, and accuracy suffers.

The biggest criticism the two-hand underhand shot receives is that it is used only on the free-throw line, and has little or no value in the field. A player can utilize his practice time better by using the same free-throw style for his set shot, thus deriving twice as much benefit from the same amount of time and effort.

Mechanics of the Underhand
Free Throw

The feet are placed slightly more than shoulders' width apart and even with each other. The toes are pointed slightly outward and the knees are slightly bent. The important point is to provide a balanced but comfortable base for the shot.

Fig. 5-1: The two-hand underhand free throw.

The ball is held between the fingers of both hands. Both the thumbs and fingers point toward the floor with the thumbs about four inches apart and at approximately a 45-degree angle to each other. The arms are extended downward in front of the body in a relaxed position so that the ball is held in front of the crotch.

Sighting of the target area is the same as for the other shots. Concentration is absolutely essential, and peak concentration must be reached at the moment of release.

The shot is initiated by a slight cocking of the wrists and a bending of the knees. With a forward swing of the arms and a straightening of the legs, the ball is released toward the basket. An upward extension of the wrists and fingers is important for good follow-through and the resulting backspin on the ball. If the follow-through is made correctly, the ball will be released from the rear of the hands.

The jump-shot free throw

I have seen more and more boys shooting their free throws by using the jump shot. I feel this tendency will continue to increase as long as the jump shot remains the most effective shot in basketball. Please note, I said "the most effective shot," not "the best" or "the easiest." I believe that, because of its tremendous success and effectiveness, most players practice it more than the other shots; therefore, they become more proficient with it than with some of the easier shots that could be used on the free-throw line. If a player has more confidence and success with this shot, he should be encouraged to use it.

There is little doubt, however, that when both feet are on the ground, it is easier to control the flight (and thus the accuracy) of the ball, just as it is easier to shoot at a stationary target than at a moving one. I have heard, and agree with, the old saw that, under normal conditions, "the fewer moving parts, the less chance for error." I believe this theory can be applied to shooting a basketball, particularly on the free-throw line.

Hal Greer, of the Philadelphia professional team, is a perfect example of a player who uses the jump shot for free throws instead of one of the other styles. Hal never uses a one- or two-hand set shot in a game, therefore he seldom practices them. Instead, he spends most of his time working on his deadly jump shot, and many feel he shoots it quicker and more accurately than anyone else in the game today. He uses this same shot on the free-throw line with equal success.

Two-hand overhead free throw

This old and distinguished technique has almost completely disappeared. I mention it only because it has always been one of the most beautiful and stylish shots to be seen. It still retains a sentimental attraction for me and for many others who consider it a real treat to watch.

Those who developed it would hold the ball high over their heads in what appeared to be a passing position. During a game they could either make a swift pass or a fast shot from this position (see Figure 5-2), and it definitely offered some outstanding advantages. Some of the all-time greats who used this particular style on the free-throw line were Bones McKinney, Carl Braun, Jack Coleman, and Frankie Brian. All of them used the overhead shot as well from the field as at the free-throw line.

General Free-Throw Hints and Techniques

Every player has his own pet techniques for shooting free throws; however, there are certain basic principles that can be applied to all styles. Because the basic mechanics of the shots used on the free-throw line are discussed in Chapter 3, this section will deal with the psychological and technical aspects of shooting free throws.

Fig. 5-2: The two-hand overhead free throw.

(1) Throw with rhythm and smoothness

I firmly believe that rhythm and smoothness are the key to successful free-throw shooting, assuming, of course, that the shooter is using the proper fundamentals. Golf instructors always stress that the swing should be very smooth and executed with a definite rhythm. This also applies when shooting a basketball, especially on the free-throw line. Any movement that is hurried or jerky will definitely handicap accuracy and control.

(2) Train yourself to concentrate

As in all sports and activities, a successful basketball player must learn how to think as well as how to go through the motions. He must learn to concentrate in order to reach his highest potential. When a player is fouled, and is awarded a free throw, he must immediately start concentrating on the execution of the shot. If he just walks up to the line and thinks, "I hope it goes in," he will undoubtedly be shooting far below his maximum ability, and he will probably have a tendency to tie himself up psychologically.

(3) Learn to relax and be comfortable

Any player who does not feel relaxed and comfortable will not reach his highest degree of efficiency. This is a very common observation that applies to free-throw shooting. If the player feels cramped or tied up, his confidence and control will suffer, and many unnecessary misses will result. Correct practice methods and mastery of the fundamentals are the answer to this problem. Each player should pretend he is shooting the crucial or winning free throw every time he shoots a practice throw. He should experiment with different techniques and methods in order to discover his most relaxed and comfortable position at the free-throw line.

(4) Establish a definite routine

The necessity for each player to develop a good

sound routine is one of the most abused phases of shooting free throws. Too often I have observed potentially good free-throw shooters merely go through the motions, without establishing a good pattern that would regulate their thoughts and actions before shooting. It is important for each player to realize that he will be shooting free throws under different conditions each time. One time he might get fouled when he first enters the game and while he still feels fresh and strong. The next time he might get fouled near the end of the game, when he is very tired. Therefore, he should work on a routine that will help him feel the same way each time he steps up to the free-throw line, regardless of the circumstances. There are numerous methods for doing this: (a) take a few deep breaths; (b) bounce the ball a few times; (c) waggle the ball before shooting; (d) take a comfortable stance before receiving the ball from the official, and so on.

The main point here is that the player must use this same routine in practice as well as in the game, so that he gets the same feeling every time he shoots.

(5) Take advantage of 10-second time limit

The main thing a player should learn about the 10-second rule when shooting free throws is neither to shoot too quickly nor to pose too long. A player can sometimes become too deliberate and lower his accuracy by standing or "posing" in one position. This usually results in his shooting short of the basket or his intended target.

Of course, a rushed shot—where the player doesn't take enough time—will also hamper accuracy. A player should learn to use that amount of time which best suits his style and form when shooting free throws.

(6) Don't have too many
thoughts before shooting

A player can lower his proficiency simply by trying to cover too many things at once just prior to shooting. The time to think and work on weaknesses or check points is during daily practice sessions. Probably not more than one or two fundamentals should be in the player's mind just before the free throw. This does not contradict the idea that a basic routine should be established: such a routine is physical whereas concentrating on additional check points is a mental process.

This rule compares favorably with correct golfing methods. Most golf instructors and pros advocate that the player have a single thought when he actually starts his swing; usually this thought involves the determination to keep every motion as smooth as possible. The thought is applicable to shooting free throws as well.

(7) Learn to keep head
as still as possible

Another golf fundamental that certainly applies to shooting a basketball is the necessity for the shooter to keep his head still. Arnold Palmer has written that keeping the head still while putting is probably the most important factor in that phase of the game. Obviously, shooting a basketball requires more body action than putting a golf ball; however, the principle of holding the head as still as possible is equally applicable and will help to improve accuracy at the free-throw line.

(8) Keep ball straight

Several techniques for sighting the target area and aiming the ball were discussed in Chapter 2. The technique that has helped me the most—particularly on the free-throw line—has been that of keeping the ball aimed straight for the middle section of the hoop rim. If the ball strays to one side or the other, the chances of its going through are tremendously reduced. . . . But *any* technique a player can develop to ensure a straighter shot is valuable.

(9) Line up ball properly

There is a distinct advantage in lining up the ball in a similar position for each free-throw shot. Extra confidence can be gained by placing the fingers either across the seams or parallel with them each time a shot is attempted.

The player should also make sure his hands and the ball are as dry as possible each time he shoots. This can become a problem with those players who perspire a lot in an overheated gymnasium. The player can wipe his hands on his shirt, pants, or socks before shooting, or he might ask the official to wipe off the ball first or ask him for permission to use a towel.

(10) Walk slowly to the free-throw line

Often a player will miss a free throw just by not being ready to shoot when he receives the ball from the official. Therefore, he should walk slowly to the free-throw line in order to prepare himself mentally and physically. If he rushes to the line and does not prepare himself thoroughly he will surely perform far below his peak potential.

Free-Throw Coaching Methods

Use your best shot

Coaches should recommend that players use their most accurate shot for free throws. This is particularly necessary for those players who have not yet developed a sound style. If a player is proficient at a two-hand set shot, he should use a two-hand set free throw. For instance, Dolph Schayes, one of professional basketball's truly outstanding players, is a master at the two-hand set free throw. I strongly concur with those coaches who feel it is a waste of time to teach a player one type of set shot and another type of free throw. A player has to be fundamentally well positioned to score on a long outside set shot. This means that he should be using his best shot and, if he uses this same shot on the free-throw line, he is receiving twice the benefit every time he practices it. If a player shoots a one-hand set and then uses a two-hand underhand free throw, it will take him twice as long to practice both shots, and the chances are he won't achieve his maximum accuracy with either one.

A big difference between the set shot and the free throw is that the shooter has 10 seconds in which to shoot the latter, whereas a set shot has to be executed much more quickly. However, the mechanics of the two shots are identical, and the player saves a lot of time by learning to use the same shot for both situations.

If a player has already achieved an accurate free-throw style, the coach shouldn't try to change it—no matter what (or whose) fundamentals or techniques it may violate. There are many successful unorthodox performers in all sports; basketball is no exception.

If a coach feels justified in changing a player's complete style, he should work much longer with the boy on form and fundamentals, rather than allowing him to join the competition which is so important to practice sessions. The new technique will feel unnatural to the boy; therefore, he must be able to devote his full attention to perfecting it. Whether or not the shot is successful is of minor importance now. . . . If the player is trying to learn a new style and he is constantly being bested in foul-shooting contests by teammates, he will soon become discouraged and lose confidence.

Make minor adjustments

Basically, the point I am making is that if the boy has developed a fairly successful technique but is using some improper fundamentals, the coach should make an adjustment in his form rather than completely change his style. If a coach tries to rush such a change, he may destroy the player's self-confidence and sense of timing. The boy then will usually become uncomfortable and tend to "cramp up." A slow, gradual adjustment gives the player a feeling of comfort and also bolsters his morale.

For example, the boy who holds his elbow too far out from his body while shooting is in an unnatural position and is releasing the ball incorrectly. But it is more successful to have him practice bringing his elbow in little by little than to try to force a complete correction all at once. The coach should always explain the reasons for any change he advises so that the boy will understand why such a change will aid his form.

Set a percentage goal

The coach should set definite free-throw percentage goals for each player. Conscientious players who often practice by themselves do not always have the advantage of competing against teammates. This can be compensated for by setting individual goals during practice sessions. If a boy is working on free throws, he should have a definite goal in mind, and make a bargain with himself not to quit until he attains this predetermined goal. For example, the player who is an 80 per cent free-throw shooter should set a definite number of attempts and not quit until he has shot them at an 85 per cent clip. This method helps to maintain interest and concentration so vital for developing the player's abilities to their full potential.

Demand improvement

Coaches must constantly strive to motivate all their players to improve their free-throw accuracy. This may be best accomplished by making free-throw practice interesting and competitive. There are many excellent practice drills and methods. One of the best methods for getting players interested and concentrating on each shot is to divide the squad into groups of twos, matching strong and weak shooters in each pair. Then one pair challenges another after the regular practice session is over. The winning group gets to go down and shower, but the losing group has to stay and challenge another losing group until it finally wins. I usually set the first game or round at 30, which means each player has to shoot 30 free throws two at a time. After shooting two, he then rotates with his opponents and his partner, so he is shooting two out of every eight shots taken. I usually drop the second round to 20 shots each. Then the third-round losers shoot 10 free throws each, until finally the last two players on the same team will have to compete against each other, with the loser shooting an extra 10 by himself.

I feel this system of ending practice is very valuable for the following reasons:

1. It motivates players and stimulates accuracy.
2. It gives a player a goal to work toward.
3. It gives each player a partner, someone to encourage or needle him into improving his performance, concentration, technique, and so on.
4. It simulates game conditions.
5. It creates and maintains interest.
6. It encourages and stresses more practice for the

lackadaisical shooters, and for those who are weaker under competition.

7. It employs a certain amount of pressure that is necessary to improve accuracy.
8. It promotes free-throw shooting while the player is still somewhat tired from practice.
9. It rotates turns enough to keep any one player from shooting too many in a row and developing unnatural tendencies that are not found in game conditions.

Free-throw drills and aids

Other methods I have found very beneficial for practice sessions are:

1. Right after a hard scrimmage or a running drill, I have the players spread out in even numbers to all baskets, and rotate turns while they're still tired. Each player shoots until he misses or makes five in a row. This is a good method of practicing free throws; it will serve to break up the monotony of a dull or long scrimmage. It is also better than any other system or technique for shooting free throws while really tired. All players would rather be shooting than rebounding under the basket, so they are motivated to bear down and make every shot.
2. The use of charts for free throws has many advantages, especially during the earlier part of the season. It can help tell the player and his coach if he is progressing at a normal rate, or if he should change his style or technique. It may point out that he is executing certain fundamentals improperly. The coach can use the chart for a quick evaluation of his players,

so he will know which are strong and which are weak in free-throw shooting, and how much time he should spend working on this phase of the game.

3. There is a definite advantage in having the players practice shooting free throws at a smaller-than-normal rim or target. There are many devices to fit over the normal 18-inch rim and reduce it to a smaller target. The smaller target improves the players' concentration and makes the standard rim seem relatively large when they return to it during practice or in a game.

Sharman Free-Throw Technique

My free-throw method is just an accumulation of the fundamentals advocated throughout this book. I have tried to study and analyze some of the more suitable techniques that would apply to my own style of shooting and to use them as advantageously as possible. No two players shoot exactly alike; therefore each player should try to work out a routine that suits him.

I will quickly go over my own method step by step. This will give an example of how some of the techniques mentioned can be incorporated into an individual routine that can be used each time while shooting free throws.

1. If I am fouled after running real hard or long, I always take a little more time to walk to the free-throw line. This extra time gives me a chance to catch my breath and to collect my thoughts before attempting the free throw.
2. I then take the stance I find comfortable and suitable to me, and line up in the same position each time.
3. I always bounce the ball a few times to get the feel of it, and also to loosen up my wrist.

4. I then assume the starting position, with my body and the ball held correctly.

5. I take one or two deep breaths. This helps to calm my body and respiration.

6. I always strive to achieve the same feeling each time I shoot a free throw.

7. I then waggle or wiggle the ball a few times. Because the ball sometimes feels different— slippery with perspiration, or tacky or slick— this gives me a better feel of the ball just before shooting. Like the waggle in golf just before the start of the swing, it also tends to loosen up the player and offer a smoother shot.

8. I then sight the basket and concentrate on pinpointing my target.

9. I always think about keeping the ball straight when aiming.

10. Next I make sure my elbow moves under the ball instead of staying behind it. This corrects the wrist cock for a successful release (see Figure 5-3, next page).

11. I always try to exaggerate the backspin on the ball (for a smoother, more accurate shot) by letting the ball roll off my fingertips and giving a good strong wrist snap.

12. I build up my concentration to a peak, just at the instant the ball actually leaves my fingers.

13. I always make a complete follow-through, which is necessary for maximum control and accuracy.

14. I always notice exactly where the ball lands. If I miss the basket or target, I am then prepared to make the necessary adjustments before taking my next shot. That way I do not lose confidence in my shooting—as I might

Fig. 5-3: Bill Sharman illustrates the free-throw form
which made him basketball's best shot from the
foul line.

if I wasn't aware of my error or didn't know how to correct it.

Free-Throw Shooting Drills

The key words in successful free-throw shooting are *competition, relaxation, fundamentals, pressure,* and *simulation of game conditions.* These are some of the elements that should be considered and used in free-throw shooting drills.

Some of the techniques I would like to recommend are: (1) Have each player step back off the free-throw line after each shot. (2) Rotate turns regularly so each player won't get into an unnatural groove that does not exist during a game. (3) Point out that the 10-second time limit should be observed during practice sessions and drills.

Elimination contest drill

This free-throw drill is usually most effective if held at the end of the practice period. Each player competes against another player of approximately equal shooting ability. Each player shoots 30 free throws (or any number set by the coach), two at a time. The winners can go down to shower or have free time to practice some other phase of the game. The losers must challenge another loser for a second round. This continues until every player on the team has won a match (some other penalty can be used for the losing man in the last pair). This drill can be speeded up by matching one pair against another.

Daily charts

Daily charts of each player's progress in shooting free throws can be very useful and beneficial. They let the players and the coach know who the best free-throw shooters are and let them know who needs special work and instruction. Approximately 50 shots each day is a good number to start preseason training. The charts should be posted in the locker rooms so each player can check his daily and weekly progress.

Shoot until miss

Game conditions can be simulated by having players divide up and shoot free throws at separate baskets right after a hard practice or scrimmage. One method of stimulating their concentration is to have them continue to shoot as long as they make the basket. If they miss, or make five in a row, they have to give up the ball. It is very important to group players of approximately equal shooting ability so that no one player will constantly dominate his group.

Free-throw ladder

A free-throw ladder can be fun and very useful to the players, the coach, and the team. Naturally, certain players will dominate the top spots, but letting the other players challenge for higher positions can serve to motivate them. Penalties and rewards can also be used very effectively in this method of shooting free throws. The number and procedure used can vary, and should be determined by the coach.

Individual free-throw goals

Complete concentration is always the best method of making any shot, especially free throws. If a player is practicing by himself, he should set a definite goal before he begins, and make it a habit not to quit until he reaches this predetermined number. The player should always strive to increase his regular shooting percentage by setting his goals a little higher than his average.

6

A SHOT FOR EVERY STYLE

AND SITUATION

This chapter will describe the many types of shots a basketball player should be acquainted with, and, ideally, be able to defend against. As he progresses, he should try to develop and use some of the more difficult and unorthodox shots. All the shots discussed here may be used by certain players and teams; however, no one player or team should attempt to develop every shot mentioned. They should concentrate only on those shots which fit into their own style and position. The fundamentals outlined in previous chapters also apply, of course, to these more unorthodox shots.

Two-Hand Underhand Lay-Up

This shot is used quite often by a player driving down the middle and aiming the ball for the front rim rather than the backboard. It is usually an effective way of drawing fouls. By using two hands instead of one, the player has a stronger grip on the ball so he can afford more contact and still control the shot. Therefore, when he is driving down the middle with a defender close by, he can take off a little farther from the basket. This offers more protection and less chance of a steal by opponents.

I would urge all players who drive a lot to work on this shot. It is probably a little more effective from the guard position, but it can be used frequently from the corners as well. I have seen many players drive from the corner toward the free-throw line, and—being unable to go all the way in for the easy lay-up—take off about seven or eight feet from the basket, using the two-hand underhand shot very effectively.

Twisting Underhand Lay-Up

This shot is generally used when a player is driving toward the basket and is forced too far under it by a defensive player. He is unable to take the normal lay-up and must rely on a pivotal maneuver to get the shot off. The most common situation usually occurs when the shooter is unable to shoot the ball from the side he is approaching, and must continue under the basket to shoot from the opposite side with a reverse backspin English off the backboard.

Of course there are many other positions and maneuvers in which the twisting lay-up can be employed very effectively. I would suggest that all players who do much of their scoring close to or under the basket work on this special technique. It can offer many advantages and higher scoring averages.

Today many of the superstars and All-Americans use these twisting and pivoting maneuvers. Probably the most famous performers that come to mind in this respect are Elgin Baylor, Cliff Hagan, and Tom Heinsohn (see Figure 6-1). All these extraordinary players have the necessary ability and body control required to master these difficult shots.

Fig. 6-1: Elgin Baylor executes a twisting lay-up to avoid the ever-present threat of a blocked shot by Bill Russell in the East-West All-Star game.

Buttonhook Shot

This shot is considered a half hook and half push shot. It usually sets up with the shooter facing away from the basket. When he receives the ball, he usually prefaces the shot with one or two fakes, then turns in toward the basket. He doesn't place the ball in front of him as he would in a push shot, nor does he hold it far from his body as he would in a hook. As the player turns, he releases the ball somewhere over his head (see Figure 6-2).

George Mikan is undoubtedly the most famous player to use this particular shot. He was the highest scorer of his decade; this shot was his most often-used weapon. It put him in a good position to follow in and rebound in case the ball didn't go in.

Hank Luisetti also used this shot during his fabulous career. He would drive by his man toward the basket, and if the center switched off on him, he would continue to dribble under the basket and circle back out. Most of the time defensive players would slack off when Luisetti didn't take the shot in close. However, as soon as the defense loosened up, Hank would wheel around and take the buttonhook shot from about 10 or 12 feet away. He would usually bank it off the backboard from the side angle, which offers a good target from that distance and position.

It has always been very difficult to develop this shot to a high degree of accuracy. A player has to have some extra-sensitive feel and touch to master it. It is not usually recommended by many coaches unless a boy does have this special ability to use it successfully.

Running One-Hand Push Shot

This shot is a running one-hand push shot that is

A   B   C

Fig. 6-2: The buttonhook is not quite as simple as indicated here, but the principles are fundamentally the same.

released very fast off the dribble. If the player is right-handed, he lifts his right knee and shoots off his left leg. This is very similar to the one-hand push lay-up position, and can be used very effectively from long

Fig. 6-3: This picture tells the story on the running one-hand push shot. Bob Cousy performs it to perfection.

Photo courtesy of the *Boston Globe*

range. A player must have great timing and good body balance to achieve a consistent shooting percentage. Because the shot can be executed quickly from a running dribble, it offers certain advantages. It will often surprise the defensive man, and catch him off balance.

This was one of Bob Cousy's favorite shots. I believe he used it more and achieved greater success with it than any other player in professional ball (see Figure 6-3). He became so efficient with it that players would have to overguard him to try to stop it. This would allow Bob to take advantage of them by faking the shot and driving around them for many extra points and easy shots.

Although, this running one-hand push shot can be used very effectively, it is a very difficult shot to master. It is much harder to shoot a high percentage while moving than from a stationary position. This shot is recommended only for the very advanced and outstanding shooters.

One-Hand Overhead Shot

This shot is taken almost in the same body position as the one-hand set shot. The main difference is that the ball is placed in a starting position over the head, rather than at shoulder or chest level. Probably the biggest advantage this shot offers is that the defensive man has to stand closer to the shooter, making him more vulnerable to the fake and drive. It also allows the offensive man to make a quicker pass: he can either fake the shot and pass, or vice versa—which can be very confusing to the defensive player.

The biggest disadvantage of this technique is probably that the ball is held at some distance from the eyes, making it harder to develop the maximum hand and eye coordination that is so vital for most skilled performers. However, some players have used this type of shot very successfully.

Mel Hutchins, forward of the old Fort Wayne *Pistons,* was probably the most famous and strongest advocate of the one-hand overhead shot. It was his favorite and most effective shot, and the one which helped him win All-American and All-Pro honors during his great career.

Two-Hand Overhead Shot

This shot was briefly discussed in an earlier chapter; however, I would like to mention some of its more notable advantages and disadvantages.

The body position is very similar to that in the two-hand chest shot, but the ball is held in a starting position over the head. Like the one-hand overhead shot, it allows greater protection from the defender and provides an outstanding opportunity for passing and feeding to the pivot. The two-hand release also makes it more effective from a longer range.

Although this type of shot has been used very effectively by such noted players as Carl Braun, Bones McKinney, Frankie Brian, and others, it seems to be vanishing from the basketball world, mainly because of the emphasis now placed on the running style and fast break. The proper position for the overhead shot takes a little longer to get into, and so the shot is probably better suited for the slow type of offense that was more commonly used a few years back.

Two-Hand Overhead Jump Shot

Actually, this shot was used and developed before the famous one-hand jump shot was introduced. It was probably the true forerunner of the jumper commonly used today.

It is executed almost exactly like the one-hand jump shot, except that the ball is held with two hands above the head. This shot never achieved the over-all success or effectiveness of the one-hander, but it was used a great deal by certain players during the early 1940s. Joe Fulks, who was the first of the big-time scorers in pro basketball, and Belus Smalley, who played with the old St. Louis *Bombers*, were both strong supporters and users of the two-hand jump shot.

Probably the main reason the shot never caught on or became more effective was that it took longer to get set for the jump. Also, it offered less protection from the defensive man than did the one-hand jump shot.

Tip-In Shot

This technique can be a tremendous weapon and for a team that is blessed with tall players who can jump well. One way to become a powerful winning team is to control the backboards, especially on the offensive end, where the second and third efforts can result in many extra baskets by tip-in shots.

The player must have good timing and coordination, and the ability to meet the ball at the very highest peak of the jump. He then controls the ball by pushing it back up toward the basket, while he's still in the air. The ball is not caught first and then shot, but tipped back up, as in the push shot made in volleyball. Although this type of shot or slap should be stressed and practiced a great deal by the centers and forwards, often a guard can slip in under the basket and score many tip-ins while the big men are blocking each other out under the basket.

Coaches and players should consider the value and importance of this shot, and try to develop and use it to the very utmost. There are many great players who can execute this shot very well; among them are Cliff Hagan, Tommy Heinsohn, Jerry Lucas, and Elgin Baylor.

Dunking and Over-the-Rim Shots

This specialty is reserved for the great jumpers who have the ability to spring so high that they can reach above the basket. Many times a player will have the chance to drive into the basket relatively free, and by jumping high enough to dunk the ball he eliminates almost all danger of missing the shot. He also can draw many fouls from his opponents with this technique, because the defensive man has to try as best he can to stop the shot, but the dunker is so high in the air that if any contact does occur it is almost impossible for the officials to miss it.

Two of the most famous of the players who take advantage of these over-the-rim and dunk shots are Bill Russell and Wilt Chamberlain. Both are big men with tremendous spring and excellent timing. They both use the dunk shot several times a game with great effectiveness. Bob Cousy and Bill Russell had a planned maneuver and signal they used for many years with the Boston *Celtics*. Whenever Russell's defensive man would overplay him, and try to position himself in front or beside him, Cousy would give the sign to start the play. Russell would fake, pretending he was going to go out high for the pass, and then quickly reverse his position under the basket. Almost immediately Cousy would have the ball waiting for him near the basket. Bill would jump very high above the rim, catch the ball and dunk it in one motion, before coming back down to the floor. This maneuver scored hundreds of points for Russell that he wouldn't have had without the ability and timing to jump above the basket.

Wilt Chamberlain has scored hundreds of points in similar fashion (see Figure 6-4). His technique, however, is a little different. Many times he will station himself under the basket just as one of his teammates is shooting. He will watch the flight of the ball, and

Fig. 6-4: Both Wilt Chamberlain (dunking) and Gene Wiley (defending) illustrate perfectly the incredible potential of the big man in basketball.

if he thinks it isn't going to enter the basket, he will leap up above the rim and guide the ball into the basket with both hands. Chamberlain is 7′ 1″ tall, with a tremendous reach and jumping ability. He is considered the highest jumper in basketball today. Usually, Chamberlain will receive the high pass from the guard who lobs the ball to him to set up this situation. This usually results when the defensive player tries to front him, instead of playing behind him. These over-the-rim and dunk shots are one of the main reasons why Chamberlain is the greatest scorer the game has ever seen. He has led the professional league in scoring every single year that he has been an active player. In the 1961-62 season he averaged over 50 points per game—an all-time record. In one game against the New York *Knickerbockers*, he scored 100 points—a league record.

Fig. 6-4a: Bill Russell

Step-Away Fade Shot

Although not commonly used today, this shot has been a very successful weapon for many players. I can remember playing against the great Andy Wolf, who was an All-American at UCLA in the late 1940s. I was a freshman at USC. Wolf was a left-hander and a great shooter. His favorite shot was the fade-away push shot. It was the first time I had ever seen this type of shot. He could shoot it off the drive from almost any distance. He would dribble around and, when the defensive man loosened up, he would plant his inside foot and fade backward away from the basket. Unless you are ready and looking for this move, it is very difficult to stop or block. Wolf was so effective and accurate with this type of shot, I practiced and worked on it all one summer so that I could use it the next year. Later it became one of my favorite and most successful shots.

Another player who mastered this fade-away shot was Fred Scolari. He was an All-League player for the old Washington *Capitols* when the N.B.A. was organized in 1946. Fred was my roommate during the 1950-1951 season, my first in professional ball. Scolari— only 5′ 10″—was one of the smallest men ever to play in the N.B.A. He was a great competitor and a great shooter. His best and most accurate shot was the fade-away one-hand push. He would plant the inside foot firmly and fade away, sometimes three or four feet back, shooting the ball at the same time. Freddie could also shoot this at long range and he achieved a very high shooting percentage during his career.

There are two important reasons why this type of shot is not used often today: (1) It takes the shooter away from the basket and almost eliminates him from following his shot for the rebound; (2) because the jump shot is so hard to stop or guard against, it has dominated all other methods and techniques.

I still think the fade-away push shot has some value. It could help many players who have the ability and patience to work on a variety of maneuvers and fakes.

Up-and-Under Pivot Shot

This up-and-under shot is still used quite often by the more adept pivot men. Centers who start their shots with their backs to the basket can certainly benefit by adding this extra weapon to their arsenal.

It is executed by faking a hook or spin shot. When the defender puts his arm up to block or hinder the shot, the shooter quickly lowers the ball and releases an underhand sweep shot under the outstretched arm of the opponent. The natural reaction is for the defender to lower his arm and, as the shooter comes up and under, this usually results in contact. The offensive man usually gets the benefit of the doubt and winds us with many extra free throws.

Most of the really great centers of the past few decades have taken advantage of this up-and-under shot. Two of its most effective users in recent years have been "Easy" Ed Macauley and Harry Gallatin. Both scored many extra baskets and free throws by developing this fake and shot. Both made All-League for years, and their ability to vary their shots and fakes contributed to these honors.

As a coaching point, I urge all centers and those players who shoot close in to the basket to work on this outstanding maneuver.

One-Hand Jump-Twist Shot

This shot involves just one maneuver more than the regular one-hand jump shot. The main difference is that when the player starts his jump he twists his body in the air before releasing the ball. The player usually starts by facing away from the basket. Many centers and big men who don't have a good hook shot rely on this jump-twist shot to score the bulk of their points.

Naturally, it is a little harder to use this shot and still maintain a high shooting percentage. It takes many hours of practice to develop the technique and the body coordination necessary to make it successful.

One-Hand Fade-Away Jump Shot

This is another variety of the regular one-hand push jump shot. Instead of jumping straight up, the player

Fig. 6-5: Jerry West gives an active demonstration of the fade-away one-hand jump shot.

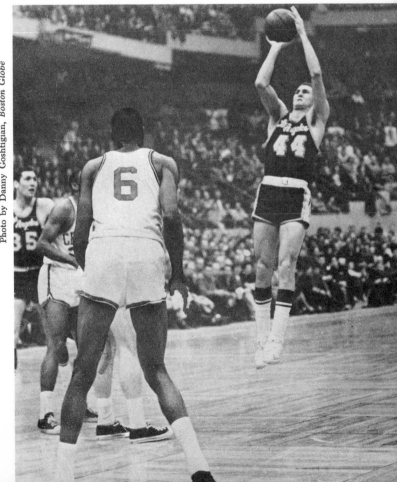

Photo by Danny Goshtigian, Boston Globe

does a backward fade-away from the basket. The fundamentals of execution (see Figure 6-5) are the same, and apply to the major steps involved in this shot. The coach should make sure that the shooter fades back in a straight line from the basket. If he fades to one side in a backward and lateral jump, he greatly increases the danger of missing the shot. He now has to judge his backward and lateral movement, plus the distance and direction to the basket. If he fades in a straight line from the rim, he eliminates the lateral movement and can judge the direction to the basket much more easily and successfully.

Paul Arizin developed this technique better than any player I have ever seen. He was only 6′ 4″ and played forward against players who were many inches taller than he. However, he had this great fade-away jump shot that was seldom blocked or stopped. Arizin twice led the entire league in scoring while he was playing with the Philadelphia *Warriors*. This was an outstanding accomplishment, for many had said he was too small ever to play forward in the pro ranks. Also, he did it when George Mikan was still playing and was usually the perennial scoring champion of the league. Most people felt Arizin would never have been able to stick in pro ball if not for his fade-away jump shot.

All the shots discussed in this chapter and in Chapter 3 must be practiced as much as possible.

There follow some drills which I have found to be interesting and helpful in producing better shooters.

Shooting Drills Used in Practice

Most shooting drills are easy and fun to teach. Most players enjoy seeing the ball go into the basket. The drills I have listed are designed to stimulate and motivate players to develop the necessary qualities a coach strives for in his team. These drills should be used mainly during the weekly practice sessions. Special emphasis should be placed on having each player use the drills that will best suit his type of game. It is important for each player to consider his shooting position on the floor, so that he may practice the shots he'll be using most of the time.

21 shooting drill

This is a shooting game, for which each team is divided into relatively equal groups. Each group uses one ball and tries to score 21 goals before the opposing team does. A designated spot on the floor is picked, and each player shoots from that spot. He receives one point for each basket made. He must retrieve his own

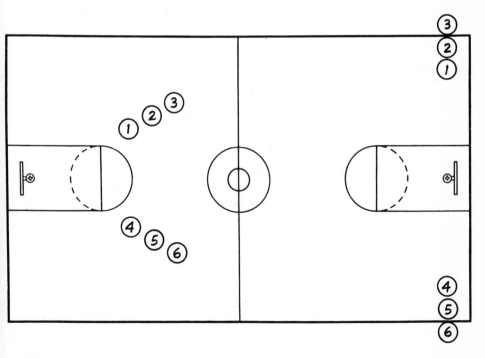

Drill A   **Fig. 6-6:** 21 Shooting Drill   **Drill B**

rebound, pass it back to his teammate, and then go to the end of his line until it is his turn to shoot again. Spots on the floor should be varied as indicated by Drill A and Drill B.

Variations of 21 game

There are two other methods of playing the 21 game. Each player may receive two shots at a time.

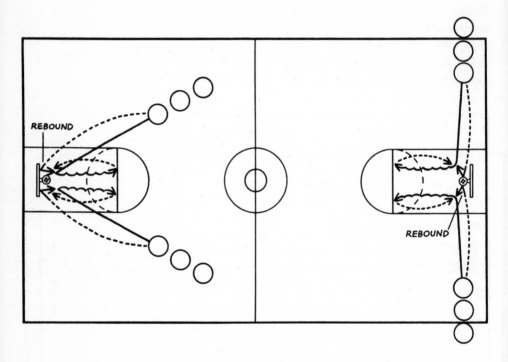

Drill A   **Fig. 6-7:** Variations of 21 Shooting Drill   **Drill B**

He takes his first shot from the designated spot on the floor, retrieves his own rebound, dribbles back to the free-throw line, and takes his own second shot Then he passes back to the next man in his group. Usually the rule is that a team must win by a two-point margin. Alternate spots on the floor should be used, as shown in Drill A and Drill B.

21 shooting and
conditioning drill

This method of playing 21 is a good shooting, dribbling, and conditioning drill that is recommended for preseason training. Each player can score a maximum of two points each time he has a turn. He takes his first shot from a designated spot on the floor, retrieves the rebound and dribbles the length of the floor. Then he must make a lay-up, after which he dribbles back and takes a jump shot from the free-throw line. He again retrieves the rebound and then

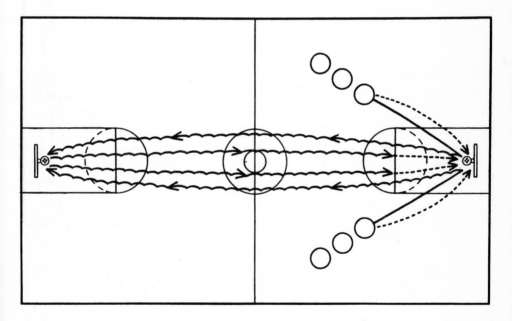

Fig. 6-8: 21 Shooting and Conditioning Drill

passes back to the next player on his team. The first team to score 21 points wins the game.

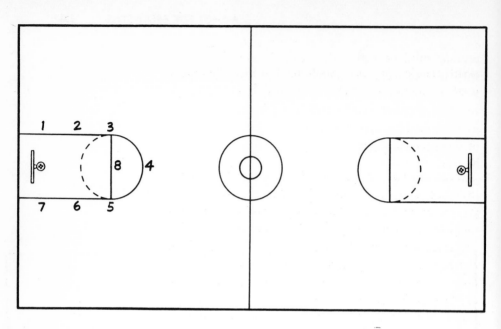

Fig. 6-9: Around-the-World Shooting Drill

Around-the-world
shooting drill

This is a good shooting drill because it emphasizes most of the shooting in the pivot and free-throw area, where the highest percentage of points is usually scored in a game. Two or more players can participate in this game. The object is to go all the way around, making a basket at each designated position, and then come back again. If a player misses his first shot at any position, he has the choice of chancing a second shot. If he misses the second try he must then start over from the beginning. If he doesn't chance a second shot he stays at that spot on his next turn. The first player to go all around wins.

Nine-hole golf shooting drill

This is an interesting and useful shooting game that borrows its rules from golf. Nine spots are designated on the floor. Each player shoots from each position until he makes the shot. He alternates turns with his opponents at each spot, until all nine positions are completed. Usually a par score is set up in advance. However, individual competition scores per spot, or medal scores that represent the total number of shots fired to complete the nine positions, may also be used. If a par for the nine holes is established, it can be used by a player practicing on his own. Breaking par can serve to motivate and improve his shooting.

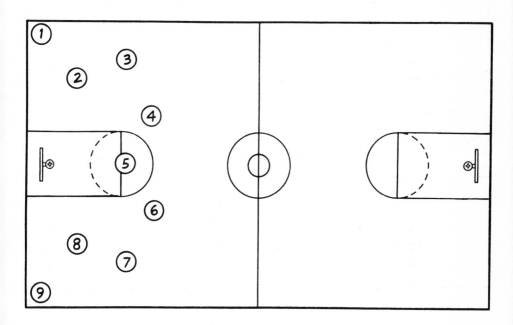

Fig. 6-10: Nine-Hole Golf Shooting Drill

H-O-R-S-E shooting game

This shooting drill, or game, is just a follow-the-leader type of contest. Each player must make the same shot as the player did who shot before him; if he doesn't he receives a letter against him. The game continues and the next man can take any type of shot

he wants until everyone—except the eventual winner
—receives all the letters of the word HORSE.

Hand-up shooting drill

In this drill, a defensive man—designated X—is
placed in front of the shooter with his arm up, and

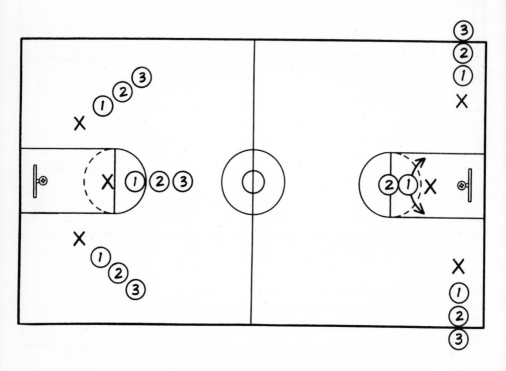

Drill A   Fig. 6-11: Hand-Up Shooting Drill   Drill B

the shooter must shoot over the defender's outstretched arms. Since the drill is designed to simulate
game conditions, it is advisable to group together
those players who play similar positions; thus they can
practice the shots and fakes they will be using in the
game. This is demonstrated by changing positions in
Drill A and Drill B.

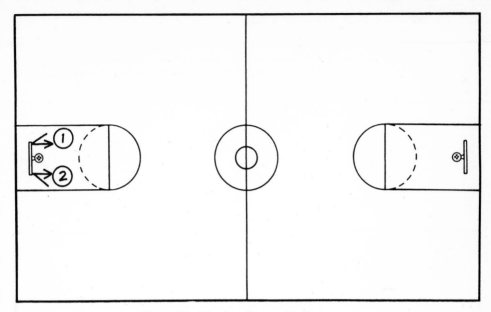

Fig. 6-12: Tipping Contest Drill

Tipping contest drill

This drill should be utilized mainly by the centers and the taller forwards. Each boy will start with a ball on his side of the basket. The object is to see who can keep the ball up on the board longest. A tip is required, which means that a player cannot catch or balance the ball in his palm. This drill is excellent to help develop timing and jumping and tipping ability.

7

OFFENSIVE FAKES THAT DEVELOP

GREAT SHOOTERS

Many times the question arises: Why is one player average, another good, and still another *great?* The answer depends on many factors. However, one of the most obvious characteristics of the outstanding players is their knowledge of and ability to use certain offensive fakes and maneuvers that usually relate to good footwork.

In trying to analyze the so-called superstars of basketball today, I have observed that nearly every one has outstanding ability to fake and maneuver the defenders out of position and leave them off balance. I'm sure all coaches have seen players who are remarkable shooters, but who haven't sufficiently developed the footwork and fakes necessary to free themselves to actually make the shots.

The one-to-one duels of a normal game usually play a vital part in determining the eventual winner. Coaches should, therefore, urge their players to give very serious thought to this phase of the game. Offensive fakes can be used in a variety of ways, and players should be coached to maneuver with or without the ball. A player will handicap himself enormously if he allows the defensive man to overplay him and he is unable to take advantage of this.

There are many rewards to be gained by developing good fakes and maneuvers. One of the most immediate results will be better and more numerous shots at the basket. A player who frees himself without the ball will receive more passes from his teammates. Any player adequately equipped to meet and challenge most of the defensive formations and strategies used today will certainly gain extra self-confidence. The ability to use these moves at the right time in the right situations is certainly essential to achieving the status of a complete or great player.

Footwork

It is necessary that a player know the different techniques involved in proper footwork. Some of the fundamentals required are starting, stopping, turning, pivoting, and changing pace and direction. These movements are important to the player in protecting the ball from his opponents and in helping him to free himself from the defensive man when he does not have possession of the ball. This will allow the passer to hit him with a quick pass for a good shot.

The importance of good footwork cannot be overemphasized. It is a requisite of an outstanding player, and it is almost impossible for any player to become a great performer unless he can execute the proper footwork skillfully and cleverly. *Footwork is the basis for all offensive fakes and maneuvers.* Every player should strive to develop the necessary moves that will free him and make him difficult to guard.

Basic footwork techniques

CHANGE OF PACE. One of the most important methods of faking or maneuvering is the change of pace, an excellent maneuver for eluding the defensive player. When used properly, it is a valuable asset that will permit a player to take full advantage of his natural speed and enable him to go by a much faster defensive man.

The offensive player has a distinct advantage over the defensive player: he knows when he will stop or start. The defensive player, on the other hand, cannot stop or start until the offensive player does. This split-second advantage of the offensive player is the chief reason why the change of pace is so effective.

The quick burst of speed and the sudden stop that are so important to the change of pace cannot be developed without proper footwork. Body balance must also be maintained, and this requires that the knees be bent. Have you ever tried to run with the knees straight? Have your players try it sometime and they will quickly see the importance of bending the knees.

The most important factors in obtaining a good change of pace are learning to stop quickly and to start quickly, learning to slow up, and learning to pick up speed quickly. Quick changes of speed keep the defense off balance and guessing. The ability to use short and long strides effectively is very essential in developing a good change of pace. An important point is to be sure to develop the change of pace with or without the ball.

CHANGE OF DIRECTION. The change of direction is an excellent maneuver that may be combined with a change of pace. It is one of the best of the moves designed to free a player to receive a pass or to get an open shot. If the defensive man is extremely fast and clever, a quick change of direction is essential. This movement is undoubtedly the basic maneuver behind the very famous give-and-go play that is often called the bread-and-butter play of all offensive moves.

The change of direction is extremely difficult to guard against because, as in the change of pace, the offensive man knows when he is going to execute the move while the defender does not. The guard must wait until he sees the move; by the time he reacts to it, the offensive man should have a step or so head start. This is all that is required to be in a good position to receive the ball.

When changing direction to the left, the player should have his right leg well bent for body balance. He should then quickly push off the right foot, coming left at a sharp angle. Then he shifts his weight to the left foot to complete the change of direction. Players must be able to execute this movement at top speed—there should be no hesitation or indecision.

REVERSE TURN. This maneuver is extremely effective for freeing a player from a tight defensive man and getting him in close for an easy scoring shot. All players should be well versed in this important movement. It is used along the sidelines, under the basket, and in the foul circle or free-throw area.

When a player receives a pass in these areas, he should step forward with the leg next to the defensive man in order to hold him off and keep him from intercepting the ball. If, upon receiving the ball, he feels the guard on one side, he should reverse the dribble into the basket from the opposite side. He should push off on the forward foot and pivot on the rear foot as he shifts his weight. After the turn it is important that the offensive man keep his inside shoulder next to the guard as low as possible so as to give good body protection to the ball on the movement to the basket. Centers and pivot men should excel in this particular move for it will keep the defensive opponent from playing so closely. The reverse turn is also a very effective maneuver for breaking clear to receive a pass.

Pivots and Turns

Pivots and turns are crucial maneuvers, and all players should learn to execute them with or without the ball. Both maneuvers are used in similar situations, and both enable the player to reverse his position or direction. The player uses pivots in conjunction with stops when he has possession of the ball. And he uses pivots and turns to protect and retain possession of the ball, to outmaneuver and work around a defensive man, to get away from the sidelines and out of the corners, and to maneuver the ball through the front line of defense.

When executing any of the pivots or turns, the player must remember to keep his body low and in balance. The knees and toes should be pointed slightly outward, and the elbows should be held wide to afford maximum protection. Again, proper footwork is essential to the successful execution of the maneuvers.

REVERSE PIVOT. The reverse pivot is used primarily to enable the offensive player to put his body between his opponent and the ball and thus better protect the ball. It is most often used at the end of a dribble.

The footwork involved is simple, but its proper execution must not be taken for granted. Countless walking violations have been incurred by faulty stops and pivots. When executing the reverse pivot, the player should come to a stride stop, moving low in a semicrouch. If he picks up his dribble while his left foot is on the floor, he should advance his right foot to brake his forward momentum and stop the stride. His left (rear) foot will be the pivot foot. He may now pivot on the ball of his left foot and move his right foot in any direction.

SIDELINE PIVOT. This maneuver is usually recommended for forwards or other players who start their moves from the corners and the sidelines. As the name indicates, the player on the sidelines should use this pivot to free himself from his defensive guard. The turn should always be made toward the sideline, because the defensive man will be to the inside, protecting the scoring area. The player should break up and plant his outside foot near the sideline. With his knees bent and his body balanced, he then pivots toward the sideline on his inside foot and cuts hard toward the basket. This sideline pivot is an excellent maneuver when a team is working reverse and backdoor plays. It is also an effective weakside move to free the player for a quick pass and shot.

RUNNING STOPS. The ability to stop quickly is almost as important as the ability to start quickly. The player who can stop suddenly while traveling at top speed is very difficult to cover. Too many players slow down when preparing to stop, and thus reveal their intentions to the defensive guards. To deceive the guards a player must be able to stop quickly when moving at terrific speed.

To stop suddenly, it is absolutely necessary that a player carry his weight to the rear and that his center of gravity be close to the floor. Good body balance is essential to proper stopping. Inexperienced players often employ a running jump stop, but this is an unnatural movement—hard on the legs and difficult to execute while retaining good body balance. The stride stop is a natural movement, and it is the most effective way of stopping quickly while retaining a good position for other maneuvers.

In executing the stride stop, the forward foot should be slapped on the floor with full traction to prevent slipping and to make the sudden stop possible. The knee of the forward leg should be well bent to absorb the forward thrust, and the rear leg should be almost straight. The ball should be held with both hands, elbows in close to the body. To best protect the ball, the player should remain in the semi-crouched or stopping position as long as he holds it. If executed correctly the stride stop helps the offensive player to protect the ball and puts him in a good position for a fake or for an easy start on the next maneuver.

THE CROSSOVER STEP. The crossover step must be mastered if a player is to be able to drive both left and right. If his left foot is his pivot foot, a player's first step toward the basket must be made with his right foot, regardless of the direction in which he drives. If he drives to the right, a simple kick-out step with the right foot is all that is needed; however, if he drives to the left, he must use the crossover step—crossing his right foot in front of his body for the initial step. In either case, the initial step must not be lateral; but it must be as much toward the basket as possible to enable the driver to get around the defensive man.

A common error for beginners is to fake right with the right foot and make the initial move left with the left foot. This results in a traveling violation. Coaches must not take this skill for granted; they must work diligently until their players master the crossover step.

Footwork fundamentals

1. Don't overfake by using footwork that is neither useful nor effective.
2. Learn to combine the different kinds of

fakes and maneuvers by using good footwork.

3. Perfect body balance and control; these are always necessary to good offensive footwork.
4. Remember that hard work and proper practice habits are vital for maximum results.
5. Always keep the center of gravity low in order to achieve maximum balance.
6. Learn to execute all movements at top speed, because that is the way they will be made during games.
7. Remember that good change of pace and direction will usually keep the defensive man off balance and guessing.
8. Let the defensive man's position determine the type of turn or pivot you will use.
9. Stay low on all pivot maneuvers to achieve quick body control.
10. Make your foot movements direct and sure, but be careful not to hesitate or to telegraph your intentions.

Various Types of Fakes

FOOT FAKE. As I have said before, good footwork is essential to good faking. Footwork is used with many different techniques, and it is an essential part of almost all faking actions and maneuvers. One of the most common fakes involves the offensive man's taking a step in one direction and, as soon as the defensive man reacts to counter the movement, quickly moving in the opposite direction. If the guard is slow in recovering from the first move, the offensive man will have an opening for a quick drive at the basket. A combination of a foot fake and a head-and-shoulders fake is often effective: it will usually take the defensive man out of position and throw him off balance. A word of caution: when using the foot fake,

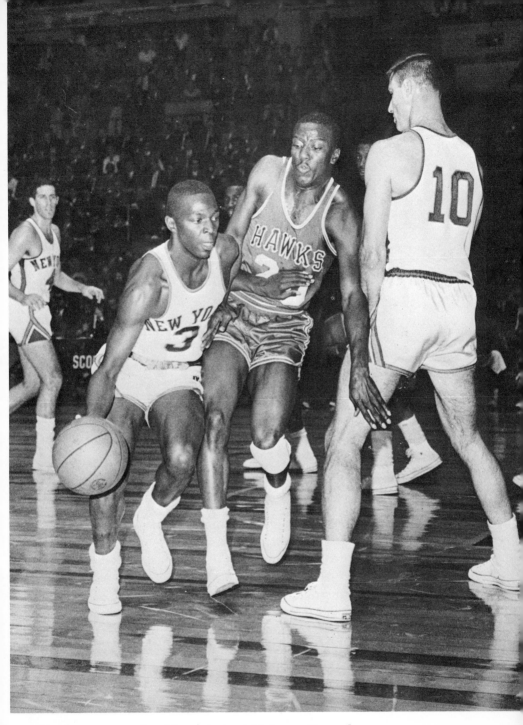

Al Butler prepares a fast fake against watchful opposition as he drives down court.

do not spread the feet too far apart, or starting speed will be greatly reduced.

BALL FAKE. The ball is almost always involved in a fake; thus the player must be able to move it quickly and effectively and keep complete control of it at all times. The ball fake is a very simple maneuver, but it is very effective when used properly. The player usually moves the ball in one direction; if the defensive man goes for it, he passes, shoots, or dribbles in the opposite direction. Timing and instinct are essential if this fake is to be effective.

EYE FAKE. Eye fakes can be very useful whether with the ball or without it. The eyes should be used in all offensive faking maneuvers. A player must learn to use good split or peripheral vision so that he does not indicate his actions or his intentions to the defense. A good offensive player must be able to look one way and pass the other; he must be able to look at a teammate and dribble in the opposite direction, and he must be able to look a defensive man in the eye and still see the whole court. Some players have a wider range of vision than others, but good split vision can be improved with practice and with effort.

HEAD-AND-SHOULDERS FAKE. One of the basic maneuvers is the head-and-shoulders fake. It is very effective whether the offensive man is facing the basket or has his back to it. The body direction is usually indicated by the movement of the head and shoulders, so it is natural for a defensive man to shift in the direction they move. The offensive player who can weave quickly in the direction opposite to that in which his head and shoulder move can often throw the defensive man off balance. Players should practice giving a good head-and-shoulders fake in one direction and quickly driving past the defensive opponent in the opposite direction. The fake must be good and the offensive player must be able to take quick advantage of any opening. Any hesitation will give the defensive man an opportunity to recover.

The head fake is particularly effective when it is used with the jump shot. By faking first with his head and shoulders, a player can keep the defensive man guessing as to when he actually is going to start his jump. If the defensive player goes for the fake, he is usually in the air and completely vulnerable when the drive begins, or the offensive player can wait until the defensive man is on his way down, and then start his own jump. Either way it is a very valuable fake that should be practiced diligently.

ROCKER FAKE. This maneuver is generally used by players away from the scoring areas. It is effective in getting past a guard for a quick drive for the basket. The ball should be held with both hands and the body should be in a semicrouched position. The player should take a step forward, with his right foot faking a drive. A good head-and-shoulders fake should be used at the same time. The left foot must be kept stationary. Next the player should rock back a full step with his right foot. This rocking movement must be done quickly and can be repeated a number of times in order to get the defensive player off balance. After executing the rocker step—if the guard fails to recover—the offensive player can shoot over him. If the guard comes up too fast, the offensive man can drive by him for the basket. The player who masters this offensive move will be extremely difficult to guard.

LATERAL FAKES. These are side-to-side fakes that are usually employed when the defensive man is crowding or overplaying the offensive player. If the defense is using a man-to-man press or whenever the offensive man cannot use the rocker fake, the lateral fakes become necessary. The object is to try to get the defensive man to lean in one direction and then to drive by him in the opposite direction. The ball is usually held to one side in order to protect it from the aggressive defensive man, who is usually trying to steal it. The main difference between this fake and the rocker fake is that the offensive man is trying to maneuver the defensive man off balance to one side rather than forward or backward.

DRIBBLING FAKES. There are various methods of achieving desired results from different types of dribbling fakes and maneuvers. Change of pace, change of direction, and other methods have already been mentioned. Probably the most common type of fake involves dribbling the ball down court and trying to drive by the opponent. As the dribbler approaches the defensive man, he should shorten his stride and his dribble. Short, choppy steps will enable him to move and fake more quickly. By bending over and shortening his dribble he will have better control of the ball, and this will help him to fake more quickly and more effectively in any direction. Head-and-shoulders fakes should be employed as the dribbler nears the defensive man, trying to get him to commit himself one way or the other. If the defensive man leans to either side, the offensive man usually has tricked him and can dribble around him in the opposite direction. As the offensive man drives by, he should take a long step with his inside foot and dribble the ball with the outside arm. This will offer maximum protection for the ball because his body will be between it and the defensive man. The ability to dribble with both hands becomes very important at this time. Also, the ability to cross over quickly—in order to drive in either direction—is essential to the success of this type of fake.

THE SWITCH OR CROSSOVER DRIBBLE. The switch dribble involves simply switching the ball from one hand to the other while dribbling. If a player is dribbling with his right hand on his right side, he pushes the ball down and across so that it will bounce up to his left hand on the left side of his body. He should be in a balanced position, with his knees comfortably bent and his head erect. He must be able to make the switch dribble without looking at the ball! The technique may sound simple, but it must be practiced for hours and hours if it is to be mastered. I have seen even professional players spend considerable time practicing this skill.

THE REVERSE DRIBBLE. This dribbling skill is similar to the reverse pivot and is used to take advantage of the defensive overplay on the dribbler. If a player is dribbling right and the defensive player overplays right so tightly that the switch dribble is unwise, a quickly executed reverse dribble can free the player for a drive to the basket. Execution is rather simple, but, again, the technique requires a great deal of practice. If the player is driving right, he plants his left foot forward and pivots on it, making a complete turn away from the defensive player. In making the turn, he swings his right leg around and toward the basket. Simultaneously, he changes his dribble over to his left hand and drives left to the basket. The swing of the right leg serves as the initial step to the basket; it also serves to trap the defensive player behind the driver.

JUMP FAKE. Because the jump shot is considered to be the most effective shot in basketball today, it becomes very important to develop a series of fakes that will enable a player to take his shot when he is in position and close enough to the basket. To achieve good fakes for the jump shot, the player must be able to fake with the upper part of his body and still be crouched with knees flexed, ready to jump at the opportune moment. The only way the defensive player can stop the jump shot is to guess when the shooter is going to start his jump and try to get up in the air at the same time to block the shot. But if the offensive player has a good series of fakes, the jump shooter has gained a tremendous advantage. Head-and-shoulders, ball, eye, and body fakes can all be used in this series of maneuvers. Practiced and perfected, they constitute one of the strongest weapons in basketball today.

Faking fundamentals

1. Learn a series of fakes and maneuvers that will cover practically all possible situations.
2. Learn to use all fakes in either direction, so that the defensive player cannot take extra advantage by overplaying one side.
3. Be careful not to become identified with certain fakes and maneuvers. A good variety of fakes should be practiced in order that they may be combined according to the situation that develops.
4. Whenever you are within shooting range of the basket and have possession of the ball, face the basket in order to keep the defensive man from overplaying you.
5. After each fake, maintain body balance and control.
6. Develop good footwork—it is essential to good fakes and maneuvers.
7. Remember that acting is part of faking; each maneuver should look like a logical reaction to the present situation.
8. Look for an opponent's weakness in certain fakes and use them.
9. Make all fakes look as natural as possible to achieve maximum deception and effectiveness.

10. Learn to react quickly after a fake has the defensive man out of position.
11. Remember that split-second timing and speed are vital to successful faking.

The Supreme Test

The one-on-one situation is the ultimate test of the complete basketball player. If a player possesses the skills described in this chapter and is an effective shooter, he should be able to consistently outscore his defensive opponent. To build a team of such players, the coach should spend considerable time in each practice period having his players working on one-on-one drills. This practice is doubly necessary in light of the increasing emphasis put on defensive basketball by so many of the nation's top coaches. Even when a player is maneuvering for a shot, he still has a slight advantage over the defensive player because he knows what he is going to do before the defensive player does. Fakes and good footwork give the offensive player the edge because the defensive player has to react quickly—and correctly—to keep up. Without good offensive fakes, even the best shooter is going to have trouble getting free for his shot. Following are some hints which should make the good shooter more effective and allow the average shooter to achieve a better position.

Important hints for one-on-one play

1. Constantly work to develop offensive fakes and fundamentals.
2. Develop an outside shot. If a player cannot hit from outside, the defense will sag off and prevent his drive.

Len Chappell

3. On receiving a pass, save the dribble!
4. Pivot and square off to your opponent; maintain body balance.
5. Develop a variety of direction fakes: fake left, drive right; fake right, drive left; fake right, left, drive right, and so on.
6. Develop the crossover step to make possible the drive both left and right.
7. Learn to dribble with either hand and without looking at the ball.
8. Develop the ability to "power" the shot around the basket. If the defense converges on the drive, take up the ball with two hands for the shot. The ability to shoot when the defense converges near the basket often leads to the three-point play.
9. Become proficient at driving the baseline.
10. Learn to pass off while on the move.

Offensive Fakes and Maneuver Drills

It is crucial that an outstanding player be able to execute these pivoting, turning, and cutting maneuvers. These drills are designed to help the player learn these important moves of the game, so that he will be able to free himself and demonstrate his shooting ability.

Hard work and dedication are necessary for quick results. A player must have enough desire to push himself through these drills if he wishes to reach his maximum potential.

Pass-and-cut drill

In this pass-and-cut drill, Number 2 passes the

ball to Number 1. Then Number 2 tries to fake the defensive man X and cut by Number 1 for the hand-off and the shot or drive to the basket. Number 2

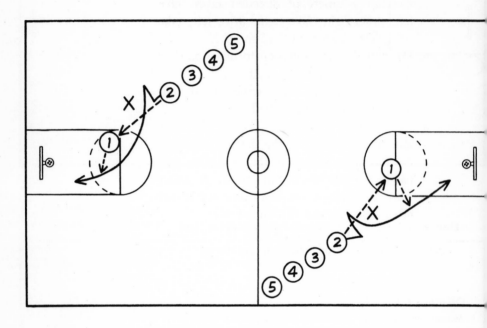

Drill A   **Fig. 7-1:** Pass-and-Cut Drill   **Drill B**

has the option of cutting outside or inside of Number 1 as illustrated in Drill A and Drill B.

Two-man weave-pivot

In this drill, Number 1 dribbles forward 10 to 12 feet, stops, and gives a head-off to Number 2, who cuts by. Number 2 then dribbles another 10-12 feet, makes a complete dribble pivot and change of direction, and hands the ball back to Number 1. Both players continue this drill the full length of the court. When one pair is about halfway up the court, the next pair should start right behind them.

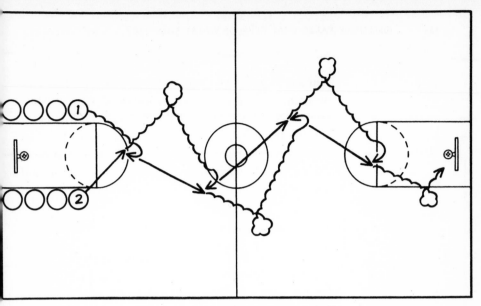

Fig. 7-2: Two-Man Weave-Pivot Drill

Drill A   **Fig. 7-3:** Give-and-Go Drill   **Drill B**

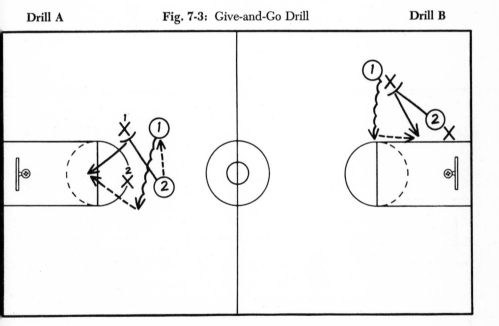

Give-and-go drill

The give-and-go maneuver is one of the oldest, yet most effective, maneuvers in basketball. In Drill A

Number 2 passes the ball to Number 1. He then goes over and sets a screen on Number 1, who dribbles around Number 2. When 1 and 2 switch, Number 2 has the inside position and breaks for the basket, and receives a pass from Number 1. In Drill B, the same maneuvers are made, but from a different angle and position.

One-on-one—three-man drill

This is a regular one-on-one drill, where the offensive man (Number 1) tries to score against the defensive man, X. The third man, O, is used as a release man and also an alternate (to simulate game conditions as much as possible). Number 1 is allowed to pass to O twice, if he wishes, before taking a shot. This gives Number 1 the practice of passing and re-

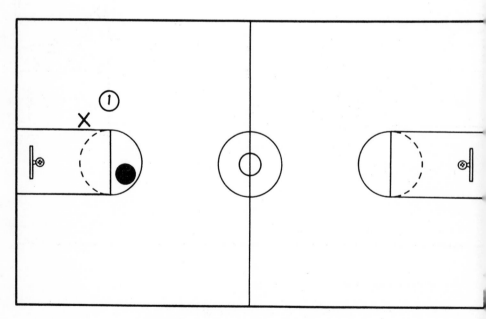

Fig. 7-4: One-on-One—Three-Man Drill

ceiving the ball before shooting, and encourages him
not to take bad shots. If Number 1 scores, he keeps
the ball and stays on offensive. If he does not score,
then the three players rotate positions. This drill can
be used in various ways.

Pivot-and-turn relay drill

In this relay drill, each boy dribbles the length of

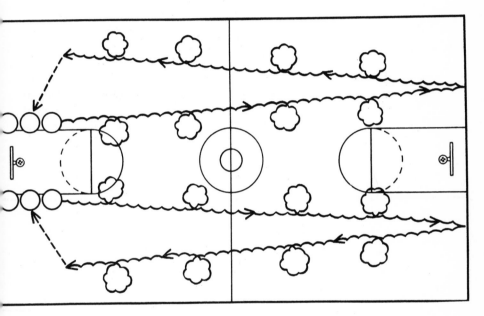

Fig. 7-5: Pivot-and-Turn Relay Drill

the floor and back. Each time the coach or the as-
sistant blows the whistle, the player with the ball
must stop and make a complete pivot before he can
continue.

8

BREAKING THE SLUMP

Skilled performers in any sport sometimes experience slumps during their careers. No matter how great they are, their proficiency cannot be maintained at peak level constantly. It usually rises and falls in very unpredictable patterns. The reasons for these slumps vary. Some slumps are caused by mental stress; others, by physical factors. Sometimes a player will fall into a slump for no apparent reason.

Because it is inevitable that all athletes will eventually experience these subpar performances, or so-called slumps, it is important that all players understand the fundamentals of their particular sport or skill. With this knowledge, they can analyze and adjust their techniques to compensate for or correct whatever may have caused them to drop below their normal proficiency level.

I have seen many younger players miss a few shots and then begin to worry themselves into a slump. An older, more experienced player who has a deeper understanding of the game can analyze his mistakes and do something about them; he will soon adjust and return to peak performance. Many times this knowledge will make the difference between an average player and a good one or a great one.

I have personally gone through many different stages. In high school and the early years at college, there were many occasions when I'd miss my first few shots in a game. Because I didn't know how to adjust to the situation, I would sometimes remain in a shooting slump for two or three games afterward.

In my later years with the Boston *Celtics*, I studied and practiced the fundamentals of the game and was able to overcome most slumps much more quickly. I also learned and practiced certain techniques that would help to prevent these deficiencies. Most of these techniques were developed through the trial-and-error method. Some were learned from coaches, players, and other personnel surrounding the team who offered ideas and suggestions.

In all fields, anything that is usable or successful is usually written down and published. I hope some of the ideas and techniques I have suggested here will be helpful and valuable to others, so they won't have to spend as much time experimenting to find the methods best suited to their style of play.

The old saying, "An ounce of prevention is worth a pound of cure," can certainly be applied to basketball. Mental and physical preparation can help to avoid or to eliminate many unnecessary shooting slumps.

Methods of Preventing Slumps

Hard work and practice

When a player is shooting below par and feels he's

entering a slump, or already in one, he should practice harder and longer. Often a minor change in stance or position can help by offering him a slightly different grasp or "feel" of the shot. No doubt the largest factor involved in slumps of any kind is loss of self-confidence. If your style of shooting doesn't feel right, then the results usually won't be good either. Therefore, take some extra shooting practice to restore this lost confidence. Also—work to change your mental attitude: sometimes a new train of thought can snap a player out of a shooting slump. Possibly a change in your thought while actually in the process of shooting will help to increase efficiency.

Don't overpractice

On the other hand, a player who is shooting well probably should not practice as long as he normally would. I have heard, for instance, baseball players say that they take only a few swings during batting practice when they are hitting well. They reason that, if they're in a certain groove, too much practice could throw off their timing. This applies as well to basketball players. When a player is shooting well, extra practice is neither advisable nor necessary.

Avoid worry

I have spent many anxious moments and days worrying about a crucial game. While this is natural enough, it can become a very bad habit and should be corrected. I remember talking about this to Dolph Schayes, now coach of the Philadelphia 76ers, and he agreed wholeheartedly. Schayes felt that too many ball players would, habitually, rise too early on the day of a big game, that they would come to the auditorium too early that night, and that, therefore, they would experience a letdown before they actually started the game. Because such fretting can become a hazard, a special thinking routine—as well as physical routine—should be set up for the day of the game. Some of the methods that worked best for me were listening to music, reading, and other similar hobbies. What is needed is something relaxing but interesting enough to keep your mind occupied.

Bob Cousy, who used to receive a tremendous amount of fan mail, would save it to answer on game days, and this would keep his mind occupied and off the game. Frank Ramsey, who has always been involved in many business ventures during the off season, would usually spend many hours of the day of a game looking over his books and paperwork. Bill Russell would spend a great deal of time and money on one of the most complete model train sets imaginable. He would often work on it, and build additional units, extra settings, and so forth, on game days.

I remember one of the *Celtics* telling me that the best way for him to get his mind off basketball was to let his monthly bills pile up and then pay them all at once on the day of the big game. This would usually shake him up so he would completely forget about the game. I tried it, and he's right. It shook me up—however. I stayed shook up during the game as well, and had a real bad night. This is one method I don't advocate, although the theory behind it does apply.

Another very successful method is painting. Tom Heinsohn, of the Boston *Celtics* and Gene Wiley, of the Los Angeles *Lakers*, both use this method quite often. They enjoy it, and they have become outstanding artists. They derive double benefit by using these talents on game days.

Diet and Eating Habits

There is little doubt that proper diet and eating habits are essential if athletes are to perform at peak level. I have heard some players say, "I didn't eat well today," yet they played a good game. Naturally, this can happen occasionally, but it's just like the athlete who says, "I can drink or smoke and still play well." The fallacy of this statement lies in the fact that he probably would have performed even better had he followed the proper training rules.

I will not attempt to outline the "best" diet, but I will suggest some of the meals and types of foods that best suited my daily routine. Naturally, this list can and should vary with each individual. The preparation of certain kinds of food, such as meats and vegetables, can be important also. Intervals between meals and before games should be seriously considered. These important details should be worked out with the individual player, the coach, the trainer, and the family doctor.

I had the privilege of rooming with Bob Cousy for eight years while playing with the *Celtics*. Cousy preferred to eat his big meal later on game days than I did. If we were to play at 8:00 P.M., he would usually eat his main meal at about 4:00 P.M., whereas I always felt better and stronger if I ate at about 2:30 P.M. However, I would usually have something—Jell-O, a cup of soup or hot tea—around 5:30 P.M. so I wouldn't go on the floor feeling hungry.

Another part of Cousy's routine on game days was to order almost any type of food that he liked best or that most satisfied his appetite. Of course this is a theory to which many dietitians adhere: they argue that your own body system will dictate what is best for you. I usually had a more standard meal,

which often consisted of broiled steak, roast beef or
lamb chops, with very little bread, butter, or potatoes,
no milk (after breakfast), a salad or some green
vegetables, and a light sherbet or pudding for dessert.

On the whole, however, a player should work out
food habits and eating routines that suit him as an
individual.

Advantages of pills
and tablets

I have always been a strong believer in the use of
proper pills and tablets—vitamins, nutritional supplements, salt, and other types that are recommended by
team doctors and trainers. These pills have proven
themselves to me in many ways: preventing bad colds
that can lead to other serious aftereffects. Vitamins
and nutritional supplements can compensate for certain deficiencies that sometimes arise on road trips,
when the team is unable to follow a regular eating
routine. Salt tablets can provide the salt needed in
the muscle areas when a player perspires heavily during a very strenuous game. Dextrose tablets also offer
certain advantages to a player and team. They can be
taken before games and between halves.

Many forms of food can serve to prepare a player
physically and mentally and help to prevent possible
slumps. The *Celtics* during my years with the team
used plain chocolate bars, hot tea with sugar, oranges,
honey, and similar items. Edward "Buddy" LeRoux,
the *Celtics'* trainer, who is one of the most skilled and
conscientious trainers in sports today, has always
stressed and made available such helpful items to the
team at all times. He has set up a special training
table right in the *Celtics'* dressing room, with hot tea,
certain vitamins, nutritional supplements, salt tablets,

and so on, always available. Each *Celtics* player has his own tea cup. Of course, some coaches feel these are minor details which contribute little toward winning or toward preparing players for a game. But I have always felt that minor details will win some ball games, especially the close ones. I would also like to point out that these so-called minor details might be one of the major reasons why the *Celtics* have won the over-all league championship in the N.B.A. for the past few years.

Proper Rest

Proper rest is vital to good shooting and top performance. The importance of rest cannot be overemphasized. I know of no way a player can start a slump more quickly than by sleeping too little.

On the other hand, a player should not sleep too much—especially during the afternoon of a game. Inexperienced players sometimes sleep too much, and inexperienced coaches sometimes allow them to do so. I have found, as have others, that if I sleep longer than an hour and a half before a game, my system slows down and I cannot perform at capacity that evening. Too much sleep seems to drain me of my normal pep and reaction speed. Nevertheless, a nap—in bed if possible—of one to one and a half hours some time during the afternoon of the game will help the player to relax and rest physically and mentally.

Some players have told me they are unable to fall asleep on the day of the game. I urge such players to lie down in bed and read, listen to music, watch television (to a limited degree, however, so that they won't strain their eyes), or do whatever else is most relaxing. These rest periods are necessary for all players because they can help them to achieve peak performance and eliminate slumps.

Refresh Muscle Memory

Shooting a basketball successfully has been described as nothing more than highly accurate muscle memory. I have always remembered that statement; it has been useful in many of the routines I have established as a player and as a coach. Just as a speaker delivers a better speech if he goes over his lines on the day he is scheduled to deliver it, so does a basketball player derive much benefit from practicing shots on the day of a game. I have always tried to shoot for 15 or 20 minutes the morning of a game—not long enough to get tired or exhausted, but long enough to refresh my muscle memory of the shots and moves I hoped to use during the game. This extra practice could easily be overdone, and there are many times when it is unnecessary; however, if done at the right time and with the right attitude, pregame practice can be of much value. The biggest benefit I derived from this extra practice session was the extra confidence it gave me.

Because of game conditions and competitive pressure, sometimes the warm-up period just before the game will not supply the necessary confidence or provide the review of muscle memory so essential for maximum efficiency.

Game-day exercises

Stretching, walking and other nonexerting exercises the day of a game have been very valuable for loosening-up purposes, especially if a player feels stiff or tight. This often occurs when he has played the night before, and his muscles are still very hard and sometimes sore.

I have found a brisk walk, combined with some minor stretching exercises, to be very helpful. The length and speed of the walk would depend on the condition of the individual involved. Like most things, this can certainly be overdone, and common sense must prevail. Probably one of the worst abuses of pregame exercise is perpetrated by the players who stand on their feet for long periods on game days (for example, going shopping). The immobile standing position will certainly deaden the spring and quickness in a player's legs. And a player will usually feel twice as tired as he would have after playing a vigorous basketball game or engaging in some other strenuous exercise.

A feeling of looseness and ease at game time can sometimes help a slumping player to turn in an outstanding game.

Pregame warm-up

Too much thinking and worrying on the day of a game can be harmful. At about the time he sets out for the court a player should start concentrating on the game, getting himself ready for the contest during this very important period. Although the coach is responsible for getting the players up for the game and going over final details and strategy with them, each player is responsible for preparing himself personally. Most professionals accept this responsibility and work very diligently to be at their very best for every contest.

that when they entered the dressing room for a game,

Coach Red Auerbach of the *Celtics* told his players he didn't want any talking that didn't pertain to that particular game. He wanted the players to think only about how to play and how to win the game.

I have usually followed Coach Auerbach's system in my own coaching methods and feel it is a valuable technique to help prepare the team for all games.

Pregame Mental Preparation

The time spent by a player in the locker room, getting ready for a game, can be very valuable. He should spend it preparing himself mentally for the task ahead of him. There should be some very serious and silent thinking and reviewing by each player before the coach calls the team together for last-minute briefing or before coming out on the floor for the warm-up drills.

Bob Cousy would always dress hurriedly and then lie down and shut his eyes for a few minutes to go over certain important details of the game.

Frank Ramsey would usually be the first player to enter the dressing room to allow himself plenty of time to get ready mentally and physically.

Many players, including myself, would always carry a card file of notes pertaining to certain teams and players that would be used for review just before game time.

Pregame Physical Preparation

I have already discussed some of the methods used to prepare physically for a game. However, last-minute details along these lines are very important. Proper equipment that fits well can be a factor in increasing efficiency while performing. Tightly fitting jerseys can sometimes bother a player enough to throw him off his normal shooting routine and into the beginning of a slump. Socks that don't fit properly can sometimes cause blisters and impair footwork. Pants that fit too tightly can handicap normal breathing.

Proper care of injuries is also an important factor in maintaining efficiency. If a player is hurt, the trainer or the doctor should check the injury instantly and use all necessary caution. The taping of ankles and other parts of the body that are vulnerable to injuries can also help to avoid loss of playing time and un-necessary slumps.

The length of the pregame warm-up drill is usually decided by the coach. However, each player should learn what is best for his own personal style, and adjust to it. One player might need more running to loosen up, where another player should concentrate on the shots he uses at his own position and not waste time and energy on shots he will seldom use. If a tall boy is playing the pivot, he will receive little benefit by going out and practicing 25-foot set shots. In a normal situation, a player should start out by running, and then jump enough to feel completely loose. Then, alternating with another player or play-ers, he should practice each shot he intends to use during the game until he makes it two or three times in a row. After going over each shot in this manner, he should have the necessary confidence and feel or touch to start the game.

Methods of Overcoming Slumps

Now that we have discussed some of the methods of preventing slumps, I would like to mention some of the techniques I have found helpful to overcome shooting slumps after they have already started. The restoration of confidence is usually the prime goal. This can be achieved in many ways. Here are some of the methods I have used and would like to suggest.

Take only good shots

One of the quickest ways of going into a shooting slump is to start taking bad shots. Conversely, one of the quickest ways of breaking a shooting slump is to start taking better shots.

When my shooting fell below par, I always worked

a little harder and usually waited a little longer for a real good shot to start each game. I found that if you hit your first couple of shots in a game, it would help to restore the confidence required to carry you through and get you back on the beam.

Change strategy

I have found that a change in strategy can be helpful in breaking shooting slumps. If I was missing regularly with my outside set shot, I would try to drive more or work in closer for short jumpers. If I was hitting a poor percentage of my jump shots, then I would try to work for other types that might be more successful.

Vary fakes and maneuvers

Sometimes a player will unconsciously fall into a stereotyped game or pattern. He may be using the same fakes and maneuvers too much, so that the defense can actually anticipate most of his moves. The ability to anticipate moves gives the opponent a tremendous advantage and allows him to overplay his man. This is one factor I would always consider first in trying to correct a shooting slump. When I wasn't receiving a normal amount of good shots, this would often turn out to be the reason.

Notice where the ball is missing

Notice where the ball is missing on the rim. This has always been a key to improving shooting habits and correcting slumps. If a player knows where his ball is missing on the rim, then he can make the necessary adjustments to correct his aim. But if the player is missing and doesn't know *where* he's missing, then he is unable to help himself correct his faults. I would always aim at the back center of the basket to start a game. When I was not hitting this intended target, I would usually be missing consistently in the same area. So after two or three misses, I would have a pretty good idea of how to compensate for the error and still not lose a great deal of shooting confidence.

Don't let crowd upset you

Many players become upset by a big crowd. I'm sure this is a very natural tendency. We are all more emotional when there are bigger audiences. If a player can learn to control his emotions, he can use the extra energy they provide to great advantage. If he lets it get out of hand, it can surely weaken his performance and possibly start a shooting slump.

The best method for me in combating this problem was to concentrate on the game rather than on the crowd. I always found enough things I should be thinking about, instead of worrying or thinking about how the audience would react.

Ignore razzing

Sometimes players have been pushed into shooting slumps by spectators who continually ride or razz them. Some fans seem to derive personal satisfaction and pleasure from this sort of yelling. Because basketball is a spectator sport and is usually supported by the paying customers, it is their privilege to holler and yell. But those players who seem to be seriously upset by this must learn how to adjust to it and accept it as part of the game.

The most helpful statement regarding these situations came from Bones McKinney, my first coach in professional ball, who said: "The fans will only get on the good players." If you're not outstanding, they won't holler at you. *That's* the time to start worrying! I always remember this and it always seemed to help me play better when someone in the crowd started razzing me.

Have a visual image

A visual image of the ball going into the basket can be helpful in breaking shooting slumps. This can be achieved by forming a mental picture of how the ball feels and looks. This always had a very positive effect on my shooting. I have also heard this theory mentioned and used by many golfers.

Avoid standing

I have often said that too much standing is a very bad habit, that will, under normal circumstances, lead to many problems. If a player learns to adjust his game with good movement, he will usually receive the benefit of an extra half-step or a full step on the man who is standing. This will often allow him to achieve a position for better shots, instead of being forced into a bad one.

Eliminate waste efforts

Waste effort can be a prime reason for shooting slumps, and should be eliminated insofar as is possible. One of the worst abusers of this role is the player who doesn't bend his knees enough, especially when he is getting ready to receive the ball for a shot. If he is still in an upright position when he catches the ball, he has to take extra time to bend low enough to drive or shoot. If he is already in a crouched position when he receives the ball, he will save time and effort because he will be ready immediately to drive or shoot. With this technique a shooter will often have the extra time necessary to make a good shot. He will not have to rush his shot and thus miss it.

Review shooting fundamentals

In talking to some 25 or 30 outstanding players and coaches concerning shooting slumps and the best methods of overcoming them, I received one answer most often: "Go back and review shooting fundamentals." If a player has a thorough knowledge and understanding of these fundamentals, he can usually analyze his own mistakes and correct them quickly.

He can also usually avoid the danger of a prolonged slump. In the next chapter I discuss some of these fundamentals and how they have helped me to overcome shooting slumps.

9

CORRECTING SHOOTING
FAULTS

How many coaches have had some player come up to them with the plea: "Coach, help me with my shot, I'm having trouble hitting"? I am sure that all of us have heard this plea at one time or another. Often the correction of a fundamental error solves the problem; at other times, more detailed study of the player's techniques must be made.

A knowledge of common shooting faults is invaluable for the coach in working with his players on their shooting fundamentals. In this chapter I will discuss the most common shooting faults and suggest some ways of correcting them. The faults are as follows:

1. Off-balance shots
2. Improper grip
3. Failure to follow through
4. Improper target sighting
5. Poor footwork
6. Improper elbow position

7. Improper ball position
8. Poorly timed release
9. Improper arc or flight of the ball
10. Hurried, jerky shots

Off-Balance Shots

It is relatively easy for a coach to see whether or not a player is on balance when he is shooting. On set shots, check to see if his center of gravity is too high or too low. On the jump shot, make certain he jumps straight up, rather than laterally, forward or backward. Make certain the lay-up is being high-jumped rather than broad-jumped.

To correct or guard against off-balance shots, have the team pair off, each player working with another of the same position. Have the players take turns and check one another for body balance.

Another good drill can be set up by placing three chairs close together in a U-shape somewhere near the free-throw line. Have the players drive into the pocket formed by the chairs and shoot jump shots. The player who is not jumping straight up for his shot will jump into the chairs as he comes down. This will make him very conscious of the vertical jump.

Improper Grip

To grip the ball properly, whether for shooting or for passing, the player must control the ball only with his fingers; he must not touch it with his palms, as many young players do. Handling the ball with the palms leads to fumbling and poor shooting. An improper grip usually puts an unnatural spin or rotation on the ball. A ball properly released has a good back-spin.

One of the best ways I know of to correct a faulty

grip is to use the fingerless glove. These gloves may be purchased at a sporting goods store or may be made by cutting the fingers off an ordinary pair of gloves. Practicing with these gloves will soon make the player aware of when he has his palms on the ball, and he will quickly see the necessity for gripping it with the fingers.

Under another method, the coach passes the ball to the player. The player quickly puts the ball in shooting position and holds the position until the coach checks his grip. This should be repeated several times daily.

Failure to Follow Through

Failure to extend the arm completely and snap the wrist and fingers downward in a complete follow-through is a very common cause of poor shooting. Without proper follow-through, the desired backspin cannot be achieved and the shot is likely to be jerky. Lack of follow-through is particularly harmful in a pressure situation: i.e., at the free-throw line late in a close game.

I have found several techniques to be helpful in improving the follow-through:

1. *Wrist passing.* Divide the squad into pairs; give each pair a ball. Players take turns passing to each other. They hold the ball in the shooting hand and, with the opposite hand, grab the forearm of the shooting hand and hold it in position. They pass the ball by using a flip of the wrist only. This emphasizes the wrist snap of the follow-through.

2. *Wall shooting.* Have players sit on the floor, about four feet from a wall, with legs spread for balance. Have them shoot the ball as high on the wall as possible. They will find that the better the follow-through the higher they can get the ball on the wall.

3. *Chair shooting.* Divide the squad into pairs; give each pair a ball. One player shoots while seated in a chair at the free-throw line. The other player retrieves the ball and returns it to the shooter. After a few shots, players exchange positions. Because no help comes from the legs, the player must have good follow-through if he is to generate enough power to get the ball to the basket.

Improper Target Sighting

The importance of proper target sighting has been stressed throughout this book. Players guilty of improper sighting are usually guilty of improper shooting concentration as well, for the two fundamentals are closely related.

The coach must make certain that each player knows where he is aiming when he takes a shot. He will often find that the player is just "looking at" the basket rather than sighting a specific target near the back rim.

I am a very strong advocate of target sighting without the ball. Players should stand in different areas on the floor and concentrate on the basket, picking out the exact target area that should be sighted from each area. Then they should attempt to carry these mental images into actual play.

Another method that helps to develop target sighting and concentration is to have the other players harass the shooter. Waving of arms, shouting, and other distracting actions can be very helpful in developing the ability to sight and concentrate properly.

When working with a player on his hook shot, I have found it very beneficial to place a small piece of tape over the spot on the backboard which he should be sighting. The player shoots at this spot daily for two weeks. At the end of that period, he has become conscious of this spot, and he will continue to sight it even after the tape is removed.

Poor Footwork

It is not uncommon to see players whose stance is too wide, whose weight is thrown onto one foot, or who are guilty of some other footwork fault. Because all shots start from the feet, improper footwork produces bad shooting habits and reduces accuracy. Footwork is essential to good body balance and control, and directly affects many of the related fundamentals of shooting.

Those players guilty of poor footwork must be identified and the necessary corrections made. A good teaching method is to have players walk into their shooting positions in slow motion. By doing this they can understand the value of having their feet in the correct position. Also, when they shoot with their feet in an unaccustomed position, they will quickly see the importance of the foot position to the shot.

Improper Elbow Position

The position of the elbow is so important in shooting that if it is incorrect many other fundamental errors arise. The most common error is to point the elbow out from the shoulder at about 45 degrees from the intended line of flight. From this position it is very difficult to "raise" the elbow in starting the shot and, consequently, a flat shooting arc will usually result. This position also restricts the wrist action needed to release the ball properly, and creates an unsteady elbow.

Correction of this fault is difficult and requires diligent practice. Usually the player has become accustomed to shooting in this manner and any other feels uncomfortable. Best results are obtained when the elbow is moved into proper position—gradually. Have the player shoot with his elbow moved two or three inches in toward the line of flight for a few days. When this position becomes comfortable, have him move his elbow in again. Continue to do this until he can shoot comfortably in the correct position. I repeat: correction of this fault is difficult and requires a great deal of practice; however, the proper elbow position is so important to good shooting that every effort must be exerted to achieve it.

Improper Ball Position

The two most common errors in regard to ball position before shooting are: (1) shooting off the shoulder, and (2) shooting from behind the head.

Shooting off the shoulder: Players guilty of this fault place the ball just above the shoulder and to the side of the ear before shooting. The habit is usually acquired when the player is young and just beginning. Lacking the strength to get the ball to the basket from in front of his body, he moves it to his shoulder and "shotputs" it into the basket.

Use a medicine ball to help correct this fault. After showing the player the correct ball position, have him hold the medicine ball in this position and "shoot" it to you. The heavy ball accentuates the feel of the new ball position and also increases the strength of his arms and wrists. Next, give the player a regular basketball and require that he shoot close to the basket, using correct ball position. Keep him close to the basket for several days and then allow him gradually to move farther away until he can shoot smoothly from outside, using the new ball position.

Shooting from behind the head: Players guilty of this fault place the ball completely above and behind the head. This forces the elbow into a position almost on the same plane as the ball and makes it almost impossible to "raise" the elbow in initiating the shot. Instead, the ball is shot with an excessive forward movement of the forearm. This forces the elbow forward and down and results in a flat or low-arc shot. A common cause of this fault is the effort to prevent the ball from being blocked.

The methods recommended for correcting the behind-the-head position are the same as those used for correcting the off-the-shoulder shot. In addition, the coach can stand beside the shooter and hold his hand directly over the shooter's head. If the ball is brought back too far, it will strike the coach's hand.

Poorly Timed Release

This is an error common in the jump shot. Players guilty of this fault fail to shoot the ball at the height of their jump: they shoot either on the way up or on the way down. This poor timing increases the difficulty of the shot, for the player must allow for the upward or downward movement of his body as he releases the ball. If the shot is released on the way up, the tendency is to overshoot because of the momentum of the body. If the shot is released on the way down, all the power for the shot must come from the arms and wrists, and thus the shooting range is decreased.

To correct this fault, have the player "shoot" without using a ball. As he jumps into the air and simulates all the basic movements of the shot, make certain that his arm motion and wrist snap come at the height of the jump. After he has gotten the feel of this new release, have him shoot close to the basket and observe him carefully. Do not allow him to move out farther from the basket until this new timing feels natural to him and he is achieving some success.

Improper Arc or Flight of the Ball

It has been shown mathematically that as the arc of the shot is increased the size of the basket area through which the shot can go is increased also. The advantages of higher versus lower arcs were discussed in Chapter 2, in which I recommended the medium arc—especially for beginners. High-percentage shooting, however, may be achieved with either a medium or a high arc. The height of the arc—or lack of it— becomes a problem when the shot is so flat as to go almost straight for the basket. This reduces the size of the basket area (relative to the shooter) so much that high-percentage shooting is virtually impossible.

The low-arc shot is usually caused by improper use of the elbow. Remember, when the shot is initiated, the elbow must be raised before the forward motion of the forearm and wrists begins. The flat-trajectory shooter does not raise his elbow; instead he uses his elbow only as a hinge, thus making the shot almost entirely with his arm and wrist.

Two drills particularly helpful in improving the arc are wall shooting and chair shooting; both were also recommended for improving the follow-through. Success in either drill requires that the elbow be raised. When using these drills, the coach must emphasize the importance of raising the elbow, and instruct the player to "feel" his elbow rise every time he shoots.

Also helpful is a device called an Arch-Builder, which hooks on top of the goal. The player must shoot over it to get the ball into the basket. The flat shot will not go in. Place the Arch-Builder on a side goal and require the flat shooter to shoot on that goal every day until his arc improves.

Hurried, Jerky Shots

Hurried, jerky shooting is primarily a matter of poor timing. The player simply has not mastered the fundamentals required for the rhythmic shot that produce maximum effectiveness. Therefore, the individual must not only learn the fundamentals; he must also learn *when* to shoot.

The same type of drill may be used for improving the timing of the shot as is used for improving the timing of the release. In addition, the counting method so successful in golf can be adapted for use here. To help the shooter keep rhythm, the coach can count for him, "one, two." On the count of "one," the shooter goes up for the shot; on the count of "two," he shoots the ball to the basket.

10

SHOOTING STRATEGY

Quite a number of situations occur during the course
of a basketball game in which the coach must make
a quick but intelligent decision. Often this decision
will mean the difference between victory and defeat.
These decisions are a phase of the multitude of
offensive and defensive maneuvers referred to as
strategy. Because the term *strategy* is rather inclusive,
I will limit my discussion here to those strategic situations involving shooting.

Philosophy

The coach's philosophy dictates the shooting strategy employed by his team. If he believes in the run-
and-shoot game, his team will strive to obtain as many
shots as possible during the course of the game. On
the other hand, if his philosophy centers around the
control game, his team will be far more concerned
with the type of shots taken rather than the number.

The method of handling crucial situations, such as "freezing" the ball or "playing for one," will also be influenced by this philosophy.

Regardless of the coach's philosophy, two important truths remain constant:

1. The coach must establish his basic philosophy in his own mind so that his decisions can be made quickly, intelligently, and without any uncertainty whatsoever.

2. The coach must make certain that his squad clearly understands this philosophy and that it is sold on it.

If a coach attains these two essentials, he will have the proper foundation for employing a game-winning strategy. The clear establishment of his philosophy in his own mind will lend authority to all his coaching techniques. A squad that not only understands this philosophy but also believes in it as well will be far better prepared to execute the desired strategy.

When to Shoot

A knowledge of when to shoot is an important mental skill that must be developed. Coaching philosophy varies greatly here, ranging from the quick shots of the fast-breaking, high-scoring game to the patient shots of the cat-and-mouse control game.

Because I was fortunate enough to be a part of Boston's devastating fast-break team, my own philosophy is centered around this type of game; however, in my own coaching, I insisted that my players not "force" the shot at the end of a break attempt. Unless the offense outnumbers the defense, or at least has a three-on-three or two-on-two situation, a team does not have a fast-break opportunity. A player who shoots the ball when he is outnumbered by the defense, unless he has driven for a lay-up, is forcing the shot and is not playing percentage basketball.

When to shoot is largely determined by when a player obtains a *good* shot. For a shot to be considered good, it must meet the following requirements:

1. It must be a shot in which the player has achieved proficiency.

2. It must be taken while on balance and in a smooth, rhythmic motion.

3. It should not be taken when tightly guarded unless a fake or offensive maneuver can reduce the effectiveness of the defense.

4. Team rebounding position and defensive balance must be available.

When a team is outmanned, it should resort to a control game and play for the high-percentage shot. The outmanned team seldom can expect to cope with opponents on the backboards; therefore, it will be at a definite disadvantage in a fast-breaking game.

Defense Pattern Affects Strategy

One of the things that will determine shooting strategy is the type of defense used by the opponents. During the initial phase of the game, cutting maneuvers should be used to determine whether the defense pattern is man-for-man, zone, or a combination of both. Once the type of defense is discerned, the appropriate attack pattern must be used.

The type of shots taken, as well as the method of obtaining these shots, will vary from the man-for-man defense to the zone or combination defense. More passes should be made before the shot is taken. Because each pass requires the zone to shift, the more passes that are made, the more defensive movement becomes necessary. As this defensive movement increases, the zone has a tendency to spread out and weaken itself in the middle; therefore, patience is a definite virtue when attacking the zone.

The alert coach can often use a substitution to increase outside shooting ability when attacking a zone. Often a team may possess a reserve who is a good outside shooter but whose offensive maneuvers are too weak for consistent scoring against a man-for-man defense. The specific talent of this player can best be exploited when attacking the zone or combination defense.

Attacking the press

The shooting strategy involved in attacking pressing defenses will be determined by the game situation. If the press is met late in the game, with the pressing team behind in points, a conservative type of attack should be employed. Keep the middle open and go for the lay-up shot. Do not take the outside jumper, whether or not it would normally be a good shot.

During earlier stages of the game, this conservative shooting strategy cannot be employed. Emphasis must be placed on attacking the defense: drive for the basket, get the lay-up if possible, but take other types of shots when they are good. The point is to remain *poised*; do not allow the defense to force a hurried, jerky shot.

Freezing the Ball

The freezing game can be divided into two types: (1) the delay game; (2) the freeze. The delay game is used when several minutes remain in a very close game. It is often used against the zone defense to pull the defense away from the basket and make possible easy lay-up shots.

The freeze game is normally used in the last two or three minutes of a close game. It is used to "put the game on ice"—i.e., to keep the ball until time runs out, if possible.

Definite attack patterns are used in both situations; however, shooting strategy varies with each. In the delay game, the object is to force the defense into making a mistake and allowing a lay-up or medium-range jump shot. The objective of the freeze game is to keep the ball as long as possible; only the unmolested lay-up shot will be taken.

Several key principles are important when freezing the ball:

1. Players who do most of the ball handling should be both good ball handlers and good free-throw shooters.

2. Crisscrosses of players with the ball involved must be avoided in order to prevent double-teaming by the defense.

3. Cross-court passes must be avoided.

4. Both offensive rebounding position and defensive balance must be maintained.

Playing for One

The strategy of playing for one shot just before the end of the period is very sound. When the game is divided into quarters, an advantage of several shots can be obtained by successfully employing this strategy. If a team gets the ball with 20 seconds to go, it gains no advantage by scoring on a quick shot and allowing the opponent also to score just before the end of the period. On the other hand, if a team gets the ball with five seconds remaining, they stand to pick up a two-points-or-better advantage.

A team using this strategy must keep the ball moving until there are approximately 15 seconds remaining, then set up the offensive pattern. The shot should be taken when there are five to eight seconds left in the period. This will allow time for an offensive rebound if the shot is missed, but not enough for the defense to take the ball down court for a shot. It is equally important that the players be coached not to foul in this situation.

Free-Throw Shooting

It is very important for the coach to be able to pick out the strong and the weak free-throw shooters on both teams. During a close game, or when an intentional foul situation is to be set up, the coach should have his best free-throw shooter handling the ball. It is also important for this free-throw shooter to shoot all free throws that result from technical fouls. If the defense finds it necessary to foul an opponent, it should make certain that only the poorer free-throw shooters are fouled!

The Last-Minute Situation

A coach's major contribution to a team usually is made in practice. However, his biggest contribution to actual game strategy can come in the crucial last minutes of a close contest.

A team must be prepared to freeze the ball, press for the ball, and execute other offensive and defensive maneuvers. Alert use of these maneuvers can often mean the difference between winning and losing. It is in these last minutes that a team's time-outs become most valuable. Therefore, the wise coach will attempt to save at least two time-outs for the last few minutes of the game.

The most crucial strategy in these situations involves special plays for obtaining a last-second shot that can win the game. Any number of plays can be used to obtain this shot; however, it should be a play that has been perfected in practice and preferably one that has not been used before in the game.

One way to handle this situation is to ask each boy on the team to write down his favorite play, and also what play he would prefer to use to take the last-second shot. This should be done before the regular season starts. This practice gives the coach a better understanding of how each boy feels about different situations, and what to call and expect when they do arise. It gives the players more confidence in themselves and in the play. They will also tend to strive a little harder to make it work, because it was mainly their idea. Naturally, the coach will usually make or suggest certain alterations, but he should try to make the player feel it is his own idea.

If the opposing team has a particularly weak defensive player, this method gives the coach an option on how to take advantage of him with a last-second shot.

There are several factors to consider in regard to the last-second shot:

1. Eliminate unnecessary passes.
2. Accelerate team movement so the defense cannot overguard each player or position on the court, such as sagging or two-timing, and so on.
3. Remember that good timing is a necessity.
4. Be alert for proper execution of signals and assignments.
5. Be aware of time remaining in the period.
6. Maintain defensive balance.
7. Provide for rebound position if the shot is missed, and allow time for a second or third effort.

II

This chapter is devoted to the results of personal or written interviews with some of the stars of the N.B.A. Throughout this book I have referred to various aspects of shooting, and to physical and mental conditioning. I would like to share with the reader some first-hand discussion on these topics from Len Chappell, New York *Knickerbockers*; Richie Guerin, St. Louis *Hawks*; Tommy Heinsohn, Boston *Celtics*; Bailey Howell, Baltimore *Bullets*; John Kerr, Philadelphia *76ers*; Bill McGill, Los Angeles *Lakers*; Frank Ramsey, Boston *Celtics*; Guy Rodgers, San Francisco *Warriors*; Dolph Schayes, Philadelphia *76ers'* coach, and Jerry West, Los Angeles *Lakers*.

I asked these stars to answer the following questions:

1. How do you prevent and overcome shooting slumps?
2. How do you correct bad shooting habits?

3. What conditions affect your shooting?
4. What do you consider to be the most important element in good shooting?
5. How do you control emotions and nervous tension before a game? During a game?
6. How do you mentally prepare for a game?
7. How do you physically prepare for a game?
8. How do you psychologically prepare for a play-off game?

How Do You Prevent and Overcome Shooting Slumps?

HEINSOHN: "During practice, I start all over again by getting the feel, first of the lay-up, then of the medium jumper, and then of the long jumper. I try to work my way out farther and farther from the basket. I have someone watch to see if the arc of my shot (which gives me the most trouble) is high enough. Then I make a conscious effort to look at the basket before I begin to go into the shot. (This can also be a problem.)"

CHAPPELL: "I watch films of shooting and try not to think myself into slumps. I practice a little harder and try to get a new spirit for the game."

GUERIN: "Actually, I feel that there is no way to prevent shooting slumps. But a way to overcome them, I think, is to get as much shooting practice as I can, whether it be on my day off or the afternoon of the game. A shooting slump gets to be more 'mental' than anything after a while. If I practice and hit consistently, my mental approach is improved."

HOWELL: "I know of no way to prevent it, but I wish I did. . . . Perhaps staying in a happy frame of mind and enjoying the game will help to prevent slumps. I think it's bad enough to worry about having a slump or to expect one, because this readies your mind for a slump, and most of the time it *does* start. I think almost all shooting slumps, especially on the pro level, are mental, rather than physical. To overcome shooting slumps I like to have about 30 minutes of solitary shooting for a couple of days. Also it helps to have a teammate permit you to shoot over his outstretched hands at close range."

KERR: "Constant practice on the shots that I have been missing and, during practice, taking shots that I would normally shoot—half-court sets or hooks."

McGILL: "I find the best way to prevent a shooting slump is to have my confidence very high at all times and to keep it high."

RAMSEY: "I wish I had the answer to this. I try to go back to the fundamentally correct way of taking each shot and I check my present method against it. Hands on side of ball rather than behind it, jumping forward instead of up, taking eye off the basket—and then practice, practice, and more practice."

RODGERS: "My shooting slumps come every year and sometimes last too long. I try to work harder on other parts of my game (defense, playmaking, and rebounding). And I try to take the good shot. Of course, you must have confidence. Usually when your shots drop you have your confidence. If I'm having a shooting problem, I just practice a little overtime."

SCHAYES: "I try to prevent shooting slumps by practicing as often as possible on shots I would normally take during the course of the game. If I find myself in a slump, I have what I call certain check points (eye stays on hoop, follow-through, finger control, and so on) that I go over to see if maybe one of these is being neglected during the act of shooting."

WEST: "1. Concentrate.
2. Take the right kind of shooting practice.
3. Don't overpractice.
4. Take a day off when you feel tired."

How Do You Correct Bad Shooting Habits?

HEINSOHN: "By practicing until I get back into the groove on all the shots I use. I have an unorthodox shooting style (which some coaches might call bad shooting habits), but when I feel the rhythm of the shot I don't seem to have a problem."

CHAPPELL: "1. Watch films.
2. Work on follow-through.
3. Practice, practice, practice.
4. Work harder on other parts of game, and shooting will come naturally.

GUERIN: "A good way would be to have a film of myself if possible. I also talk with people who know my shooting style and ask if they have noticed me doing anything wrong. I used to talk a lot about shooting with a great shooter, Carl Braun."

HOWELL: "I concentrate on the elements of good shooting while I am practicing alone. Also, I find it is a big help for the coach to continue to play me during a slump and not add to my worry by jerking me out of games."

KERR: "Usually bad shooting habits come with faulty footwork. Thus I work on foot position in my shots."

McGILL: "By constantly going over the bad habits I have picked up and practicing the correct method."

RAMSEY: "Don't take any shots that you wouldn't normally take in a game. Approach each practice shot as if you were behind with three seconds left to play. Never goof around in practice."

RODGERS: "I practice only the good shots. I try not to take the long shot, especially the one over 18 feet. I practice shooting my jump shot from the foul line. I shoot going towards the basket; I do not fade away."

SCHAYES: "I think bad shooting habits are something that you get into unconsciously, or else from trying shots that are just not within your capabilities. Everyone has certain strong points in his favor and he should use these and continue developing them to the best of his ability."

WEST: "The proper steps in correcting bad shooting habits are: (1) when you practice, practice correctly; (2) don't experiment when you know you might pick up something that's not fundamentally right."

What Conditions Affect Your Shooting?

HEINSOHN: "Of course, injuries, as well as various defensive tactics of the other teams, affect my shooting. If I am physically tired, I notice it affects my jump shot because I'm not able to maintain the same height on the jump."

CHAPPELL: "1. Rushing the shot.
          2. Improper follow-through.
          3. Worrying."

GUERIN: "If gym lighting is bad, it can affect distance judgment. Fan-shaped backboards affect hook shooters or fellows who bank their shots. Also, the physical condition of the player (sickness, injury) all can affect shooting."

HOWELL: "A dirty playing floor, or pressure from the defense, or pressure to shoot well to obtain personal success—all cause me to shoot poorly. Mental fatigue or apprehensions about the game also affect my shooting."

KERR: "(1) Not looking at the basket. (2) Watching the ball in flight instead of concentrating on the rim. (3) Not shooting at the peak of the jump when taking the jump shot."

McGILL: "Lighting ... defensive men ... physical fatigue ... and not being emotionally 'up' for the game —all these affect my shooting."

RAMSEY: "The physical layout of the gym (background, floor, etc.) and the condition of my body (such as sore legs or feet) may keep me from shooting as I normally would."

RODGERS: "Most of our plays start by going to the corner. To me, this is the hardest shot to make. When they lay off me I usually pinch off. And go to the foul line after going through."

SCHAYES: "A good defense, plus things like mental lapses, not being able to get up for a game, and, of course, the possible injuries that occur—all can affect shooting."

WEST: "1. Improper or insufficient rest.
2. My position on the floor.
3. My defensive man.
4. Insufficient concentration."

What Do You Consider the Most Important Element in Good Shooting?

HEINSOHN: "Keeping my eye on the rim plus the confidence, developed through constant practice, that I can make the shot. Developing a rhythm so that it is not a jerky motion but a nice smooth release. Fingertip control is also an important element."

CHAPPELL: "1. Follow-through.
2. Correct body position.
3. Concentration.
4. Practice, practice, practice."

GUERIN: "Once you have mastered the correct way of shooting, the most important element is confidence."

HOWELL: "Concentration on the basket. Forearm directly under the ball and the elbow not permitted to wander to either side. The ball must feel comfortable in the hand, and follow-through and delivery must be smooth."

KERR: "Don't force or take the bad shot!"

McGILL: "Confidence is the most important element—and also a natural shooting touch. Concentration on the front of the rim, proper elbow position, fingertip control and proper follow-through also are important."

RAMSEY: "Concentration on basket during the shot, proper timing, and taking the shot the same way each time (many people vary shots and this throws the shot off)."

RODGERS: "1. Never force a shot.
2. Never take a shot you haven't practiced.
3. Never surprise your teammates when shooting."

SCHAYES: "1. Eye on the front rim.
2. Fingertip control.
3. Follow-through.
4. Practice."

WEST: "1. Knowing who the good shooters are and the reasons for their success.
2. Knowing the proper position for hands, arms, eyes, and feet when shooting."

How Do You Control Emotions and Nervous Tension?

A. Before a game

HEINSOHN: "By trying to think of something else— i.e., by reading, going to the movies, drawing. This, however, is sometimes very difficult because I am always subconsciously aware that the game is coming up. This tension, to my way of thinking, is a good thing because it keeps me sharp and alert for and during the game.

CHAPPELL: "1. Read.
2. Talk to people."

GUERIN: "Watching TV or reading a good book helps me to relax before a game."

HOWELL: "During the past five years I experienced nervous tension only before the season openers and All-Star games, so it is hard to answer this question. I like to be excited about a game, but not to be nervous. The best way to control tension would be to think about something besides the game, but this could also be dangerous."

KERR: "1. Eat at least four hours before the game.
      2. Try to get a lot of rest the day of the game."

McGILL: "I always think of the things that I am going to try to do and know that I can do the job well. I also rest, listen to music, and go to movies."

RAMSEY: "It's impossible for a competitive athlete to reduce pregame tension, so just learn to live with it. This emotional upset is good in certain ways because it gets more adrenalin in the blood for more energy."

RODGERS: "At home I play my stereo, or watch TV. I try to get at least two hours of rest the day of the game. On the road, I try to keep a good schedule."

SCHAYES: "I get prepared a good time ahead of the game so I can be relaxed instead of rushing to the game and rushing to get taped, dressed, and so on."

WEST: "1. Rest.
       2. Read.
       3. Walk.
       4. Various routines."

B. During a game

HEINSOHN: "This can be a very difficult problem, but if I stop to think about it, I realize it's almost impossible to play a perfect game. Players are bound to make mistakes. I try to play as hard as I can, and if I make a mistake I forget it. If you play your game you do the great things just as easily as the bad. So I don't feel the tension."

CHAPPELL: "I keep my mind clear and don't worry about mistakes."

GUERIN: "Once a game starts, I don't have time to become nervous: too busy on the court. Confidence in yourself and in your teammates eases tension."

HOWELL: "By playing as hard as possible and realizing that this is all I can do and that I will not have any regrets if I have done my best. By concentrating on my desire to win and trying to play my best."

KERR: "I try to remember that any kind of unsportsmanlike emotion shown during the game could call for a technical foul or possible expulsion. This would hurt your team and put you in a position where you could no longer help the team."

McGILL: "I always try to do the things that come to me naturally, and this helps a lot."

RAMSEY: "Once a game starts, tension eases through [the exertion of] playing, but it is very hard to control tension while on the bench."

RODGERS: "When the first jump ball is tossed, I am 'straight'; I don't feel nervous [any more], but we all have our problems during games, and also before games."

SCHAYES: "Once the game starts, your instincts and abilities take over. The only thing that might happen is the possibility of a 'choke' in the closing seconds when a shot or foul shots are a must [to win]."

WEST: "1. Go through the preset routines.
2. Concentrate on the game plan.
3. Concentrate on plays that might work."

How Do You Mentally Prepare for a Game?

HEINSOHN: "By thinking about the player I must

cover and all his moves, and about the defensive man that will take me, his habits, and so on."

CHAPPELL: "I think about my weak points—but optimistically, confident that I am going to do my best and that the team will win."

GUERIN: "I think about the team we will be playing, their strong points, and what we generally do to combat them. Then I review the man I'm going to guard and the things that I have to try to do to stop him."

HOWELL: "I think about how important this victory is and how much enjoyment I get from winning. I think about the personal satisfaction involved in my team's winning and my playing a good game."

KERR: "I rest and think about the team we're playing and the type of game (free-lance, fast-break or set plays), the men I will be guarding, and the men that will be guarding me. I also get to the locker room early, where nothing but basketball will be on my mind."

McGILL: "It depends on who I am going to play against. Each game is different. I try to think about what my contribution to the team should be, and then give my all to get the job done."

RAMSEY: "I think about whom I will guard, and I go over in my mind those moves I know he will use and the proper defense against them."

RODGERS: "Sometimes I have a harder time than at other times. Against the really good teams—there is no problem. But this is our job and we must do our best at all times. Of course, over an 8-game schedule it gets tough."

SCHAYES: "If your stomach isn't full at game time, you shouldn't have any problem."

WEST: "I think about personal pride, the rivalries of certain teams and the desire to produce against well-thought-of opponents—the importance of winning in general."

How Do You Physically Prepare
for a Game?

HEINSOHN: "By trying to get as much rest as possible."

CHAPPELL: "By resting, but without a nap."

GUERIN: "I generally like to shoot for about half an hour during the afternoon before a game; I eat about four to five hours before the game, and then rest up to game time."

HOWELL: "I take plenty of natural vitamins and get adequate rest at all times. Different people require different amounts of sleep. I like eight and a half hours to nine hours each night, with a one and a half- to two-hour nap the afternoon before a game. I like to eat about five hours before game time. The food should be good quality, but the particular kind of food has no real bearing. I believe that adequate rest is more important than adequate food."

KERR: "I rest, eat properly, and tape all injuries."

McGILL: "By getting in condition and staying in condition. I try to rest and get eight to ten hours of sleep each night, and I also try to eat the proper foods."

RAMSEY: "I try for proper diet, rest, and treatment of injuries. You can't burn the candle at both ends and give a 100 per cent effort in the game."

RODGERS: "I eat the proper foods and take vitamins. I drink a lot of fluids, and get plenty of rest."

SCHAYES: "Plenty of rest the night before a game— from eight to eleven hours of sleep. I eat a good meal five hours before a game and get the required daily vitamins. I eat a little sugar or dextrose an hour before game time, and I tape both ankles."

WEST: "I try for proper rest, proper eating habits, and proper mental attitude."

How Do You Prepare
Psychologically for a Play-Off
Game?

HEINSOHN: "It's not too difficult when the season reaches this [play-off] stage because I realize it is a 'must' game. The big problem here is not to get too tense."

CHAPPELL: "Tell myself I am the greatest. I *try* to build self-confidence."

GUERIN: "Even though you're tired you give it that little extra, knowing there's no tomorrow."

HOWELL: "I concentrate on the special importance of the game; that increases the personal satisfaction gained when my team wins or I play a good game."

KERR: "I think of the team we are playing, and keep basketball on my mind. I take particular pride in playing well in clutch situations."

McGILL: "When it is down to this point, you know this is what you have been striving for all season. It isn't tough to get psychologically fired up for battle."

RAMSEY: "Play each game as if it were your last and as if your life depended on winning it. Don't joke to relieve tension—tension helps a good athlete to become great."

RODGERS: "Play-offs are different from other league games and all players are usually psychologically fired up for these games."

SCHAYES: "In important games, the crowd usually gets you going, but it is up to you to push your body a little more. I find that if you start out working hard on defense, the offense will come around, too."

WEST: "1. Team pride and achievement.
2. Awareness of the strength of your team and weakness of others.
3. Positive thinking of all players."

*   *   *

Conclusion: When the Game
Is Over

I have devoted most of this book to details of shooting techniques and offensive strategy—with the emphasis on shooting and scoring. It is my belief that inasmuch as shooting wins games, successful coaching of various shooting techniques is vital. I also feel that it is the hardest and most delicate phase of basketball to teach. I would like to make it very clear, however, that I am a firm believer in hard work in all phases of the game, and that each phase must be developed and coached to achieve success.

Bill Russell's grand slam
in basketball

Bill Russell was never a big scorer or great shooter, but he is a living reminder to all coaches and players of how great a player can become without being a high scorer. Russell has accumulated so many honors and awards it's hard to tell which is the most outstanding. Often when I'm asked to speak at basketball banquets I will relate what I call the greatest individual feat ever achieved by any player in one year. I call it the "Grand Slam of Basketball." Most sports fans are familiar with the four championships that Bobby Jones won in the 1920s, referred to as the "Grand Slam in Golf." Many are also acquainted with Don Budge's slam, and more recently Ron Laver's grand slam in tennis that was achieved with the winning of the world's four major tournaments in a single year. However, not too many people are familiar with Bill Russell's achievement in which he played a vital role in the winning of three of the world's top basketball championships—all in a single year. This grand slam occurred during the period from the end of the col-

Fig. 11-1: Pictured dramatically is one of the reasons why Bill Russell is a great basketball player—another blocked shot.

lege basketball season in 1956 to the end of the professional championship play in 1957.

Russell was a senior at the University of San Francisco during the 1955–56 season. He led his team to an undefeated season which included a sweep of the N.C.A.A. play-offs that gave them the national championship. He was voted the most valuable player of the tournament, and was a unanimous selection for All-American for the second straight year.

In the spring of 1956, Bill was selected to play on the United States Olympic basketball team which took part in the 1956 Olympics in Australia. Again he was the outstanding player and leader, guiding the team to a sweep in the competition and to the gold medal. Russell was voted the most valuable player in the tournament, and the team was proclaimed the World's Amateur Champions.

He returned to the United States in December and began playing with the Boston *Celtics*, whose season was already under way. Bill Russell then proceeded to lead that team to its first world's professional championship, to complete a grand slam which included membership on the collegiate, world amateur, and professional championships teams. There is no coincidence involved in this amazing accomplishment—he was the leader of these teams with his outstanding team play on defense and offense. Never the greatest shooter in the world, he was truly a complete player. He came to play basketball, and that after all is the key to winning in this great game.

INDEX

A

B